MARK GREGSTON

TOUGH GUYS

>>>>> AND <<<<<

DRAMA QUEENS

HOW NOT TO GET BLINDSIDED BY YOUR CHILD'S TEEN YEARS

PARENT'S GUIDE

THOMAS NELSON
Since 1798

NASHVILLE DALLAS MEXICO CITY RIO DE JANEIRO

Published in Nashville, Tennessee, by Thomas Nelson. Thomas Nelson is a registered trademark of Thomas Nelson, Inc.

Published in association with the literary agency of Wolgemuth & Associates, Inc.

Thomas Nelson, Inc. titles may be purchased in bulk for educational, business, fund-raising, or sales promotional use. For information, please e-mail SpecialMarkets@ ThomasNelson.com.

Scriptures taken from the Holy Bible, New International Version®, NIV®. Copyright © 1973, 1978, 1984, 2011 by Biblica, Inc.™ Used by permission of Zondervan. All rights reserved worldwide. www.zondervan.com.

ISBN: 978-1-4016-7756-5

Printed in the United States of America

12 13 14 15 16 QG 5 4 3 2 1

CONTENTS

WELCOME

Chances are, if you're reading this book or attending this curriculum series, you share the same passion for kids and teens that I do. I'm sure this passion has begun to usher in a few concerns about how to best meet the needs of your children as they enter into this teen world of massive exposure and powerful, captivating pressures. Whether you're a parent who has kids about to enter the teen years, a grandparent wanting to know more ways to help your grandchildren, or a parent of a teen who already is feeling the "heat of influence" from today's adolescent culture, I understand your concerns.

The greatest challenge facing parents today is learning how to continue to influence their children for good, in a time when the teen culture changes rapidly and permits (and promotes) more and more alternatives that are counter to what many moms and dads desire. It is my prayer that this curriculum series will provide a springboard for all parents to do a number of things that will help them maintain a relationship with their children as they enter the turbulent waters of adolescence. I also pray that parents will continue the godly influence on their children by maintaining relationships, developing new lines of communication, and exploring and implementing new techniques to help their children prepare for and navigate through their teen years. Here is what I hope will happen for you in this series:

First, I hope that you will gain an understanding of the current condition of teen culture and why teens struggle with their entrance to adolescence. The understanding of a situation, an influence, or a crisis can often change your approach to that situation. And a change of approach often changes an outcome, just as a gentle answer turns away wrath.

Second, I want you to have an opportunity to reflect upon your current parenting skills and strategies to see if they can improve. I'm not one of those guys that will spend all my time telling you where you've been wrong and pointing out mistakes. I'm one that merely wants to help you explore alternative approaches that may be more effective.

And third, I want to give you some sound and proven practical advice that will give you tools to effectively prepare and parent your teens through their adolescent years—tools that I utilize every day in my work with the teens (sixty of them) that live outside my back door.

So, this series is best utilized by either parents of preteens to help them in their preparation for the upcoming adolescent years, or by parents of teens to help them understand the need to shift their parenting style to accommodate the developing and changing needs of their teens. I'll also spend time flavoring this presentation with discussions and information that will help you identify key sources of conflict within your home and offer practical and wise advice as to how to overcome current or potential problems.

Listening to me is important, but not as important as a couple of things that are paramount to getting the most out of this presentation.

I would ask that in each session you bring your wisdom and insights gained from what you have read and seen, and what you have implemented in your home. Your insight as to what is happening in your family is as important as anyone else's in the group. Come ready to share what you are learning, not ready to tell others what they are supposed to be learning. This ensures that all benefit from the mutual exchange of those things that you become aware of.

The overriding benefit to getting together with others and watching a video is the group discussion that follows. You have the amazing opportunity to listen to other "ears and eyes" that, looking at the same situation, are able to share what they hear and see, perhaps something different from what you glean from the sessions. These insights are invaluable, as you will gather wisdom from others. A word to the wise: just because someone shares a story or observation doesn't mean that he or she is inviting a lecture, a pounding, or wants to hear your opinion of the comments. Be sensitive to the words of others. When words shared are met with opinions and comments, many times the person sharing feels judged, corrected, or de-valued. Work hard to make sure that each person is heard. Remember, this curriculum is an opportunity for you to learn, not a platform for you to teach.

I hope you will learn from listening to me and reading my "stuff." There can also be a real advantage in learning from the perceptions of others and embracing the hearts of those in the group. In addition, I hope this curriculum series will come to your mind throughout the week so that you can "chew" on the concepts and principles that are presented and truly hone your skills as a parent to the neatest kids in the world: yours.

The format of these sessions is pretty simple: The sessions will begin with a discussion about what you learned the previous week. You will then be given an opportunity to view the next video session and work through focus exercises (to ensure that you've gotten the key points out of the lesson), along with questions for discussion at the end. I hope you'll spend time giving your response. And of course, there will be an action point for the week, helping you apply what you've learned from the lesson.

I hope that you'll have as much fun watching and reading as we did writing and filming. And I pray that you'll build some deep relationships with others in your group as you walk through this portion of your parenting journey. The goal is to help your little tough guy or drama queen have some great teen years. You are essential in making that happen.

—Mark Gregston

INTRODUCTION – LESSONS FROM A DUCK HUNT

I swam competitively for years and even received a full-ride swimming scholarship to the University of Arkansas. I never thought I would come close to death by drowning. I never thought that was possible. Until one fateful duck hunt.

You see, every year I take a group of guys to Arkansas to spend a couple of days duck hunting. Each morning we wake early, put on waders, grab our guns, and head out to wander through waist-deep water in search of the airborne delicacies that we hope will fly close enough to us that we can take them back to the hunting lodge as our afternoon snack. Our guide directed us on safety and in particular told us, "Be extra careful while walking in the water because whatever you do, don't fall."

On this particular morning, I slipped out of the boat into the calm, frigid water in a place where I had never been before. The flooded timberland was no more than three feet deep, and I leaned against a tree hoping that my bulky clothing and the tree's bark would camouflage my presence. That way, I could surprise at least one of the millions of ducks that pass through that part of the Mississippi migration flyway.

Expert swimmer. Good hunter. Shallow water. No big deal. I spotted a duck and took a shot. My targeted duck made a splash, and I started to wade through the murky water to retrieve it. My focus was on the duck, my gun was in my hand, and I was determined to bag my first bird of the morning. It looked like it was going to be an easy task. It rapidly proved otherwise.

With one foot cautiously following the other, I soon realized I was wading through hidden toppled tree limbs, brush, thickets, and broken branches. Still I trudged on, stumbling over the hidden underwater snares, yet convinced I knew what I was doing. Suddenly I tripped on something I hadn't seen in front of me. My foot wedged between two submerged logs, and my effort to pull it out threw me off-balance. As my left side slowly started to tilt into the water, I resolutely tried to keep my eyes focused on the duck (so as not to lose it) and my right hand out of the water (so I wouldn't lose my gun). In a split second, horror stories came to mind of how many a good hunter had drowned when his waders filled with water.

Then the sensation of cold water trickling down my back, covering my waders, woke me to the realization that I was going under. I needed to react quickly or the situation was going to go from bad to worse in a heartbeat.

My focus on something I thought was important (the duck) and my determination to hold on to something I thought was valuable (my gun) were causing me to sink. I had to rethink what was important or it was going to be the death of me. I grabbed a tree with my left arm and thrust my gun under the water with my right, in order to get my balance. As water poured into my waders, I took my focus off the all-important duck, rethought the value of my gun, and embraced something that was secure enough to save my life—the tree. That cold-water experience got my attention.

As soon as I evaluated what was truly important (my life) and let go of what wasn't (the duck and my gun), I was able to loosen my foot, regain my balance, stand up, and take a deep breath. My heart was pounding, my eyes were misty, and my back was wet. As I leaned against that tree, I exhaled a sigh of relief. It wasn't until I was back at the lodge a few hours later that I realized what had really happened in those seemingly quiet waters. Even though I thought I knew what I was doing, I had almost drowned.

In a similar way, parents wade into the unknown waters of their child's adolescent years focusing on what they think is right, holding on to what they believe is valuable, and believing they know what they're doing . . . and they all too often end up in a mess.

Parents may begin to coast along as the waters of adolescence approach. Well-meaning moms and dads overestimate their parenting abilities and underestimate the influence of the submerged "branches and logs" of cultural pressure that entangle their families when the teen years arrive.

Perhaps your parenting *focus* has been on the "bagging the duck" of managing your child's outward behavior when, in fact, your child's life desperately needs to be saved. For example, maybe you've had your heart set on your daughter becoming a great piano player, encouraging her to excel, and pushing her to practice. She is learning piano, but what you may have failed to notice is that she is also experimenting with drugs after school. Or you've been cheering your son at football, dreaming about him getting a college scholarship, unaware that he has started using steroids and is experiencing violent mood swings. I had to let go of my treasured gun to save myself. What might you need to let go of to save your child?

It wasn't easy to pry my foot loose on that fateful day, and I had to let go of something *valuable* to do it. As parents, you may have to let go of some of your expectations and your plans in order to refocus on the big picture of what is truly important in order to preserve your family and your relationship with your child. The process of learning what is valuable often comes at the most inopportune time and at a high cost.

Most parents have some sort of plan for raising their children and think they are prepared. I made a plan for my duck hunt and thought I was prepared. I was a seasoned hunter. I felt, as many parents feel, that I had done it all before and was competent enough to handle anything that might come my way. When I got out of the boat and stepped into the water, I felt a great sense of confidence that it was going to be a successful day. I had walked through duck hunting water before. But I had never walked in that water before.

If I had a dollar for every time I've heard a parent say, "I never thought my child would . . ." or "We had no idea," or "I didn't see it coming," or "I thought we were doing everything we were supposed to," I'd be a rich man. Most parents believe in the goodness of their children and think, "That will never happen to my kid."

I've had more than twenty-five hundred kids live with me at our residential counseling center. It's a year-long program where we have sixty kids at a time stay with us, so we can get to know the kids and parents as we help them work through the struggles of adolescence that have come their way. In my experience with thousands of families and kids, I hold this to be true: if you don't think you'll ever face challenges when your child enters his or her adolescent years, then you don't prepare, and you won't be ready to meet the challenges when your teen needs you the most.

> It's easy to go under, even in those places where we are most familiar.

So, to help you be ready for that time, and to help your kids face the challenges they will face as they enter adolescence, this video series has been designed as an avenue to give parents a chance to review their goals, their approach, and their focus as they prepare their children for the adolescent years. Your children can mature into godly, healthy, productive adults, with family bonds remaining strong (or strengthening) against the turbulent waters of the teen years.

This is what I want you to get from this series:

1. An understanding of the current condition of teen culture and the reasons why many teens struggle through their entrance to adolescence.

2. An opportunity to reflect upon your current parenting skills and strategies to see if you can improve.

3. Sound and proven practical advice that will give you some more tools in your toolbox to effectively prepare and parent your teens through their adolescent years and share effective methods that engage your children in relationship.

I believe that if you can accomplish these goals, you will solve most problems with your teen. A common theme I see with parents is that they overestimate their abilities as parents to transition in their teen's adolescent years without any "hitches," and they underestimate the powerful influence this culture can have on their children. I hope you'll let this series be your "cold-water experience" to prepare you to effectively meet and respond to the greater needs of your teens.

Any child can be affected by culture.

I have a small sign on my desk quoting a proverb that reminds me daily of my need to reflect, ponder, wander, question, seek wisdom, evaluate, and re-strategize my thinking for what is set before me. It is a quote that has changed my life: "The way of fools seems right to them . . ." And the second part of that proverb? ". . . but the wise listen to advice" (Prov. 12:15).

I should have listened to our hunting guide and taken him a little more seriously.

FOCUS EXERCISES

▮ KEY CONCEPTS

1. Parents sometimes hold onto something they consider *valuable*, when their kids perceive it to be of little or no value.

2. What's important in the elementary school years is not necessarily *important* in a child's middle and high school years.

3. Parents should work hard to ensure that they have their eyes and heart *focused* on the right things as their children enter adolescence.

4. Most parents need to learn what's *beneath the surface* of the seemingly calm waters of adolescence to avoid *stumbling and falling* when their teens need them the most.

5. Most parents would like to avoid a *cold-water experience* to wake them up to the real needs of their child.

6. As you enter the teen years with your child, it's important to *understand* the teen culture, to learn how to *reflect* upon your current parenting skills, and to add some more *tools* to your parenting toolbox.

QUESTIONS FOR DISCUSSION

1. Can you write out your parenting focus in one sentence?

2. What hidden dangers might lie beneath the surface of the seemingly (by all appearances) calm waters of your child's life?

3. What are you holding onto that you would consider valuable in your parenting goals and strategy with your kids?

4. Is it possible those items you considered to be valuable during your child's elementary school years might not be valuable during the middle and high school years?

5. What "secure tree" would you grab hold of should you "trip" or feel yourself start to "go under"?

6. Do you feel that all parents have to have a "cold-water experience" before they see the need for gaining a deeper understanding of today's culture and wake up to the need for updating their parenting techniques? Has there been anything that's gotten your attention and caused you to refocus on what is important for your family?

7. Do you believe that the calm waters of the elementary school years guarantees smooth sailing during the upcoming teen years?

8. Do your parents know everything that happened in your life during your teenage years? What leads you to believe that you know everything that has happened in the life of your child?

ACTION POINT FOR THE WEEK

While you're eating dinner with your family sometime this next week, ask your preteens, "What's your greatest fear about getting older?" Also ask your teens, "How are the teen years different than your preteen years?" Then, share with them the concerns you have for them as they get older.

Session

2

WHAT'S SO DIFFERENT ABOUT TODAY'S CULTURE?

Most parents believe that if they just do the right things and protect their kids from all the evils in the world then their children will perform well, stay on track, and not be influenced by the pressures of their culture. Yet many who have held to this belief find their kids leaving the church upon graduation from high school, abandoning what they have been taught, and ignoring what they know to be truth.

The reality is that the culture has changed drastically from when most parents grew up and developed their parenting styles and concepts. Unaware of the effects that today's culture is having on teens, parents become frustrated when their styles don't work, and they see their teens moving further away spiritually and relationally as time passes.

The luring and enticing promises of this culture's message, as well as the alternative lifestyles that are promoted, permitted, publicized, and prevalent, are appealing to teens' normal levels of curiosity in their search for identity. The culture has shifted, and so must parents' styles of engagement with their children.

The place to start is by gaining an understanding of the effects of the current culture on teens, and embracing the idea that most of our kids who have gone astray have been enticed victims rather than willing participants.

This realization will change the way that you approach your child and turn your feelings of disappointment into understanding and compassion.

Here's how the culture is affecting our kids and influencing their lifestyles and decision-making:

OVEREXPOSURE TO EVERYTHING

With teens spending almost ten hours a day in front of some type of screen (computer, television, cell phone, electronic reader or tablet, smartphone, portable music player) accessing videos, visiting Internet sites, communicating with peers, searching the Web, listening to music, video chatting with family, playing video games, communicating through tweets, and sending/receiving photographs, is there any question about the increased amount of information that is overloading them? It's called information bombardment, and it is happening at such a rate that teens are exposed to everything imaginable. Can you think of anything that teens haven't seen these days?

Technology and the Internet have changed the face of the world, the way we all live, and the way we engage with one another.

Teens are overexposed to images and words that make lasting impressions, numb the senses, and instill new ideas. And while this exposure has a good many benefits for us all, there's no question that consideration must be given to how it affects our kids.

The sexualization of the culture cannot be attributed to just the presence of 4.2 million pornography sites on the Internet.[1] That's much too easy an answer. Porn has been around for a long time. It has flourished because

> Parents must understand the culture and the impact it will have on the life of their child.

---

[1] Family Safe Media, "Pornography Statistics," http://www.familysafemedia.com/pornography_statistics.html.

the culture has become permissive, and images have become accessible. For the teen culture it has an amazing appeal to disconnected girls who desire to have someone pay attention to them and to confused young men who long for ways to express their manhood. Imagery plays a big role in the life of teens, and seductiveness and sensuality just happen to be two of the ways that teens direct attention to themselves.

This overexposure to culturally permissive influences that are no longer controlled by parents, and the permission to explore and engage in alternative lifestyles and ways of thinking, has become the "right" of all teens longing to find themselves in a culturally eclectic atmosphere where anything goes.

LACK OF REAL CONNECTION

Those ten hours spent looking at a screen of some sort have an opportunity cost associated with the activity that very few anticipate. Every hour spent looking at a screen (except for video chatting) is one less hour spent relating face to face with someone else. I would submit to you that this lack of interaction is doing two things to teens. First, teens' lack of genuine relationship with one another fuels their drive to connect, so they go to greater lengths to get noticed and make a statement in hopes that someone will pay attention to them. They long to belong. Second, when social interaction is limited to one-line texting statements that become rapid-fire, chatter-filled responses, communication becomes "more about me than about thee," and the opportunity for "iron to sharpen iron" doesn't happen as it would in face-to-face conversation. As Ecclesiastes 10:10 states, "If the ax is dull and its edge unsharpened, more strength is needed." And that strength is usually shown in a teen's willingness to get "closer to the edge" and engage in more extreme behavior to make a first impression, be accepted, and find peers who are like-minded.

This lack of connection then creates a world where expression is welcomed and encouraged. One doesn't have to listen long to media sources to understand that many are crying out, "Won't someone just listen to me!" as if to find value in the expression of opinions. I'm reminded of the old proverb that states, "Fools find no pleasure in understanding but delight in airing their own opinions" (Prov. 18:2). Texting, social media, tweeting, and YouTube are not bad things. They provide the perfect opportunity for teens to express their opinions. However, when this style of communicating becomes their primary source of interaction, it doesn't take long to understand that the opportunity to engage at a deeper level is many times lost and plays "second fiddle" to their chosen, and oftentimes more convenient, form of communication.

There is a lack of real connection between kids.

This "great disconnect" among teens has also created a world where appearance becomes a priority, and a comparison mind-set enters a child's thinking. Value of self is determined by how many "friends" one has on social media sites or how many "likes" are given to comments and expressions posted electronically. The concern for "how I look" in front of peers takes center stage, and one's abilities, talents, character, or personality fades into a backdrop that is rarely seen or displayed. Overexposure to what others have through the Internet and media channels fuels a greater sense of entitlement and diminishes the meaning of the word *contentment*. I see teens spending more time in the shallow end of the "relationship pool," never venturing into deeper waters where value is determined by those attributes that lie beneath the surface. Perhaps you'll notice the priority of appearance in the following scenarios:

- A daughter shows a little more skin and violates her standards of modesty to attract guys or to fit in with other girls her own age.

- Your best friend's son starts using language while texting or posting on social network sites that is unacceptable to parents but welcomed in a teen's world because he wants to appear to be strong, manly, and tough.

- Your pastor's son changes preferences in music and lifestyle because he wants to disconnect with a church group that has high moral expectations and connect with another group of friends who accept him for who he is.

- A twelve-year-old niece is being made fun of by her peers for the way she dresses and now wants new clothes, a new hairstyle, painted nails, and makeup in order to find acceptance by those who ridicule her.

- Your next-door neighbor's daughter takes advantage of her photography skills and sends seductive or scantily clad pictures of herself in hopes of finding a connection . . . with your son.

Not only is appearance a priority, but performance becomes crucial. In a world of disconnected teens, "what you think about me" and "how I perform" become a poor standard of the value for one's life. Here are a few examples of some performers:

- It's the daughter who will stop at nothing to make good grades and either immerse herself into studies or learn to cheat because she feels she has to do well in school to find her value in life.

- It's your son's best friend who will fulfill the dares or push the limits with drugs and alcohol and engage in some unthinkable behavior because his friends push him into it.

- It's a young lady in your church's youth group having oral sex with a guy because sexual performance is vital to keeping the relationship.

- It's the girl who checked your groceries this morning at the local grocery store, who is encouraged by her friends to have sexual intercourse because she needs to complete her "rite of passage" into their circle of friendships.

- It's the daughter who dives into depression and now hates her parents after realizing that she isn't as talented or gifted as her parents led her to believe.

- It's the teenager who performs obsessively in athletics, band, or academics because he's deriving his value and importance from his performance rather than his love of the game or his talent.

Kids want to belong somewhere. And because shallow on-screen relationships don't offer a connection that is so desperately wanted, dependence on behavior and arenas that help teens find ways to stand out, appear right, and perform well become paramount.

OVERRESPONSIBLE PARENTS, IRRESPONSIBLE KIDS

Some parents, desiring to have better relationships with their children than they had with their parents, choose to "do" more things for their kids, instead of being content to "be" someone in their child's life.

Overresponsible parents create irresponsible kids.

These parents spend way too much time in their children's teen years wanting to please them at all cost, protecting them in every way possible, and providing everything their children want. So much time is spent doing these three things that parents fail to spend any time preparing their child for the next stage of life; thus irresponsibility and its by-product, immaturity, flourish.

Moms and Dads, your attempt to be overly responsible in the lives of your teens stifles motivation, eliminates creativity, promotes irresponsibility, and postpones maturity. I know you want a better relationship with your child, but there are better ways to develop it.

NO ONE GETS RESPECT

So when your kids hear about a few crooked politicians, do you think they question the intentions of all politicians? When they hear of teachers having sex with fellow students, does it change their concept of teachers? If a child hears about the sexual trysts of one president, do you think it changes her perspective of all who hold that office? What do you think many kids think of priests with all the reported sexual abuse saturating the news? When a child hears of a professional athlete's life failures, does it taint his image of professional athletes? How about when a minister of the gospel is sleeping with another man's wife and your teen finds out about it? Or when he hears about a Boy Scout leader who's not leading boys down the right path? Or worse, when she hears of a parent who has killed his or her own child or spouse or has abandoned the family? I wonder how a teen interprets the excessive and sometimes embellished information spouted over many news sources.

I see this shift begin to happen. Teens shift their respect for people to a respect for things and possessions, further fueling their sense of entitlement. They also don't give respect unless it is earned. And relationally, they now see "bad" before they see "good." This shift pushes them into withholding respect for authorities who potentially could be held as a source of wisdom in their lives.

LOSS OF GENDER DIFFERENCES

Teen culture is already confusing, but the loss of gender differences adds another element of bewilderment as to who they are at a time they're "trying to find themselves" and search for their own identity. They see guys getting married and politicians determining whether marriage between homosexuals is right or wrong. They hear constant debate about gender roles and lawsuits galore screaming for equality between the sexes.

Musical expression includes girls kissing each other and liking it, media portrays men as buffoons on sitcoms, and the influences of old (politicians, teachers, ministers, heros, etc.), aren't quite as influential as they used to be when their personal lives were unknown, and their exploitations were kept silent.

Kids are confused in a culture that is not giving them answers.

First, inside the heart of every teen girl is the longing to be valued for who she is and not what she can do sexually. And second, inside the heart of every teen guy is a desire to express his manhood through something more than the size of his body parts, what toys he owns, or how he performs physically or academically. Every woman wants a prince, every kid wants a hero, and every man wants to be both.

Whether homosexuality and same-sex relationships are right or wrong is not my point of discussion here. I'm just saying that the issue of gender differences is confusing for kids.

LIVING WITH CONSTANT UNCERTAINTY

Today's teens hear rumors that the end of the world is coming soon. They witness the loss of life by natural disasters that sweep across distant shores rattling islands with a death toll that is incomprehensible. They hear of war and rumors of war and watch movies at the local theater about the earth's demise. They live in a time of economic crisis and hear outspoken critics speak of the gloom of the world. They see the broken promises of jobs and positions to those who complete their education. Our government is out of money, Wall Street's volatility screams uncertainty, terrorism is a constant threat, businesses are failing, and nothing feels secure. The bombardment of information captures teens' hearts and teases their imagination, leading them to think that everything is worse than it actually is.

The response is often one of the two following statements: "I'm going to take control and make sure some things are certain in my life."

Another response is that teens give up and live a life that is entirely opposite of how they were raised—behaving recklessly and not thinking about the consequences—because whatever they do doesn't matter anyway.

So what's my point in all of this discussion about the crazy culture that teens must live in? It's confusing. That's it. And if it's confusing for any or all of the reasons I list, then it's important for parents to walk their kids through their confusion. On that path, I encourage parents to not be afraid to help their teens process their thoughts and ponderings, and to not walk as a judge and jury to tell them where they're wrong in their thinking, but as a voice that speaks truth in their confusion.

—— FOCUS EXERCISES ——

▌ KEY CONCEPTS

1. Teens are overexposed to *images* and *words* that make *lasting impressions, numb the senses,* and *instill new ideas.*

2. *Alternative lifestyles* and *ways of thinking* are now not only *prevalent*; they are *promoted, publicized,* and *permissible.*

3. Teens' lack of genuine *relationships* with one another fuels their drive to *connect* with their peers because of their deep longing to *belong.*

4. Today's teens are encouraged to *express* themselves, and that is mainly accomplished through *appearance* and *performance.*

5. Because no one gets respect without earning it, teens have shifted their respect for people to a respect for *things* and *possessions,* further fueling their sense of *entitlement.*

> Don't miss your child at the time they need you the most.

6. Every woman wants a *prince*, every kid wants a *hero*, and every man wants to be *both*.

7. Overresponsible parents spend too much time *pleasing*, *protecting*, and *providing* for their children and not enough time *preparing* them for the next stage of life.

8. Many times, well-meaning parents do too much for their teens and, in the process, these actions stifle *motivation*, eliminate *creativity*, promote *irresponsibility*, and postpone *maturity*.

9. Kids living with uncertainty either take *control* of their lives or give up, thinking that it *doesn't matter anyway*.

10. The culture has *shifted*, and so must parents' *style of engagement* with their children.

▌ QUESTIONS FOR DISCUSSION

1. At any point in your parenting have you made the comment, "I'm glad I wasn't raised in today's teen culture"?

2. How has "overexposure" affected your family?

3. What are some of those influences affecting your child that you have no control over?

4. Do you feel "caught in a bind" when permission for some behavior is allowed elsewhere, and standing your ground about what you will allow is questioned and becomes a point of conflict with your child? What do you usually do in this situation?

5. Do you feel your child is more disconnected from relationships than you were when you were in high school?

6. In what ways has your son or daughter bought into the world of appearance and performance?

7. If your child is becoming more and more disconnected from peers, how do you see that affecting him or her?

8. Do you do too much for your child?

9. Do you think that doing everything for them is keeping your children from learning to assume responsibility for their lives and maturing toward independence?

10. How would you characterize your relationship with your teen: one of respect or disrespect?

11. How do you usually handle the situation when your child has been disrespectful or has not shown respect for you or others in the family?

12. Have you seen a shift in the way that children view gender roles in their lives and in the lives of their peers?

13. How do you discuss these gender issues with your child?

14. In our teens' world of uncertainty, what do you offer that is constant and an "always" in their lives?

ACTION POINT FOR THE WEEK

If you have teens that have spent some time indicating that there are differences between the culture that you were raised in and the culture that they are living in, take them out for coffee, ice cream, a meal, or just a walk where the environment allows for discussion. Ask them what they think the differences between those two cultures are, and have some fun talking about the differences. But also acknowledge where today's culture perhaps confuses you and raises concern in your mind for them.

If your child is ready to hit those teen years and is a little apprehensive to "jump in feet first," ask how you can help him or her move into the upcoming years. Those discussions might start out with questions like the following:

- What would you say are your greatest fears about school next year?

- How do you think that life will change for you as you get older?

- Do you see friends becoming mean and more hateful towards others?

- Who's your best friend, and do you think that will change as you get older?

- Who would say that you are their best friend? What do you like about them?

- If you could change one thing about yourself, what would it be? Do you think that will happen this next year?

Let this be more of a time of listening than you speaking. Hear their hearts, and it will give you a better basis to ask more questions in the future. Eventually, they'll start asking you questions and you'll have the invitation that you've been looking for to speak truth into their lives.

WHY TRADITIONAL PARENTING NO LONGER WORKS

The rules that applied to the parenting game played long ago are no longer applicable to the new parenting game that is being played today. The boundaries have changed. The rules have been altered. The team and the uniform both look different. The idea of winning is still king, but the strategies to do so are vastly different from a generation ago. If you can't learn the new rules, the new strategies, and the new style, you'll lose for sure.

And if you try to play the game with the old rules of engagement, you'll be eliminated quickly. It's a new game. The purpose of this lesson is to help you understand that some of the old ways of tackling the issues of teen influence are actually now illegal or not allowed, or they might just get you penalized.

Becoming knowledgeable about the various influences on teens today and gaining understanding of what no longer works on the playing field of parenting teens sets up a parent into a new model of parenting that will bring success. Before we walk on the field, let's talk about and understand three parenting approaches that don't work.

———— PERFECTION IS IMPOSSIBLE ————

Parents have always wanted good things for their kids. Every parent longs for his or her kids to do well, make it in life, and be all that they can possibly

31

be. My parents wanted that for me, and I'm sure your parents wanted that for you: not perfection, but for their offspring to always strive to do better.

The difference now is that teens are constantly told they're imperfect because of the shift in the youth culture, thus causing kids to interpret parents' encouragement, holding to morals and biblical principles, and sharing of wisdom as being critical.

Bullying is a constant middle school hot topic that can destroy the self-esteem of a young person in a matter of a day. Their world of comparison shows little mercy. And the lack of affirming, "connected" relationships leaves many to have to fend for themselves.

It's not what you say, it's how you say it.

During the early years, kids think their parents are perfect. They don't see the flaws, the blemishes, and the pimples of life. You protect them, provide for them, and aim to please them—nothing wrong with those actions. But in their minds, they think you are perfect. Young girls and boys usually think that about their parents.

So these little princes and princesses enter their middle school years believing they live in a perfect world and have perfect parents. They soon find out that the world isn't so perfect. They begin to learn that the world is cruel, comments are harsh, people are mean, and not everyone is good. They're exposed to more, experience more, and encounter more than they ever thought they would, and perhaps beyond what they were trained to handle. Little boys turn into tough guys to protect themselves, and little girls turn into drama queens to be one-up in a world that is always trying to put them down. In their attempts to make sense of the world and apply what they have learned their whole lives, they come home emotionally spent and then interpret their parents' well-intentioned comments of encouragement and direction as a demand for perfection.

It's a tough spot for kids, and a tougher spot for parents, who want to encourage but feel somewhat crippled when their intentions are misconstrued and misinterpreted.

Here are some statements I've heard from teens over the past year. Would your kids be able to say any of these things about you?

- "I brought home some grades I was proud of and my mom started complaining that I could do better, I wasn't living up to my potential, and I needed to work harder."

- "I never understood how my imperfect parents always demand perfection of me."

- "I wish my parents knew that the messiness of my room was just a picture of the messiness I felt in my life. They seem more concerned about my room."

- "I remember when my parents and I had a fight over me not wanting to go to church, and they were so concerned about what others would think if I didn't show up and if we had an argument."

- "I couldn't measure up to my parents' ideal world, so I gave up."

- "I think my rebellion at home was my attempt to prove to them that they don't live in a perfect little world."

- "It's funny to me that we had the most screwed-up family in our whole neighborhood, and our yard was prettier than everyone else's. I think it was my parents' way of pretending to others that we had it all together."

- "I can't wait to leave home so I can relax and enjoy life."

- "I've considered committing suicide, and my parents are more concerned about the cleanliness of my bathroom than the condition of my heart."

- "Sadly, I set out to prove that my life of imperfection was better than their life of perfection."

- "I was sent away to get help for my emotional problems. No one in my extended family knows because my parents are scared they won't be seen as good parents if someone knew their child is messed up."

- "I thought my dad hated me because of the zits on my face. He always seemed embarrassed when I showed up around his friends, and he would make excuses to them, in front of me, as to why my face looked so bad. I remember scrubbing so hard that I would cry and wonder what was wrong with me."

- "I got tired of trying to attain something that I could never reach, so I quit trying."

- "My world of conflict with them was easier for me than living up to their world of perfection."

- "I was never good enough in my mother's eyes, so she nagged me all the time to do everything better. I rebelled and acted out just to prove her wrong and to show her that I was in control of my life."

- "Every time I saw my mom's mouth open, I shut my ears to her comments about how I was always failing at something. I think she meant well, but all I heard was, 'You're not good enough,' which is exactly what I was hearing from others every day at school."

The message of perfection fuels the attitude that appearance and performance are the priority for relationships with others. It teaches kids that acceptance, love, and engagement with others are based on what you do rather than who you are. Remember, what your kids actually learn from you is based on how they perceive you, not on what your intentions are.

AUTHORITY CANNOT BE FORCED

The second element that has changed for many teens is their respect for authority. I've already mentioned why they don't automatically respect those in authority and run the other direction when authority is forced on them.

The discipline techniques of old just don't work like they used to, do they? This isn't a debate on whether you should spank your preteens or paddle your adolescents, or whether there's merit in either. The issue here is that what once worked in parenting no longer works. Authority can't be forced.

But my suggestion is that respect for authority happens best when it is cushioned on a foundation of relationship's appeal rather than a show of authority through antiquated means that only damage relationships.

Do you ever find yourself saying these things that might be interpreted as a show of authority?

- "It's my way or the highway."
- "You do so because I said so."
- "Do as I say, not as I do."
- "As long as you live in this house, it will be done this way."
- "I don't care what you think; this is our home."
- "You will respect me . . . I'm your father!"
- "You will call your stepmother 'Mom.'"
- "I'll say what I want when I want to say it, and you'll listen or be grounded."
- "I will read and look at anything written in this house."
- "Change your attitude right now!"
- "I don't have to give you a reason."
- "It's my TV, and we will watch what I want to watch."
- "Go to your room now, and don't come back here until you say you're sorry."
- "You will go to church and you will like it."
- "You're a [whatever your last name is], so act like it."
- "Quit crying, you sissy."
- "Here are the things you need to change about yourself . . . and you need to change them now."
- "Here are the things I don't like about you."
- "I don't care whether you think I need to change . . . I'm the parent here."
- "I'm the king of this house and you will do as I say."

It's not that I don't believe in authority. I do. It's just that teens today don't respond to authority because of the shift in the influence of the culture coupled with the bombardment of information that many times eliminates any hope for respect of that authority.

Most people don't know that I have a donkey named Toy, one of the many animals that I share my life with.

Here are some ways that parents sometimes provoke their teens to anger and shut down any hope of respect for their authority:

- Setting unrealistic expectations for their age
- Neglecting their feelings or comments
- Comparing siblings
- Not listening to their hearts
- Embarrassing and ridiculing them
- Not respecting their opinions
- Showing favoritism toward one child over another
- Impatience and frustration accompanied by yelling and screaming
- Insensitivity and unwillingness to validate their feelings
- Sarcasm and name-calling
- Having too many rules and not enough relationship
- Correcting continually to the point where they don't want to be in your presence
- Being preoccupied or too busy with work or others
- Not respecting privacy and their need to have some downtime
- Having too high expectations
- Falsely accusing based on presumption rather than fact
- Always having to be right; can never be wrong
- Pretending to be perfect when they know otherwise
- Lying to or misleading them
- Breaking promises
- Overreacting instead of responding

Toy is a stubborn donkey. I can try to get her to do something, such as follow me, to listen to instructions, and to avoid something dangerous, but she has a mind of her own and often displays her obstinate nature. So when all my efforts to get her to respond to me aren't working, I find myself wanting to prove my authority by hitting her, pushing her, and yanking on her lead rope until I am worn out. What I have learned is that Toy doesn't

- Overprotecting instead of preparing them for life
- Not respecting their decisions and shaming them for mistakes
- Not respecting their desires, hopes, and feelings
- Having low expectations of child's ability to think and solve problems
- Disciplining the child in front of others
- Showing marriage conflict in the extreme
- Making a child take sides between two parents
- Inconsistency of discipline; disagreement between parents in approach
- Never trusting the child
- Inflexibility in what you believe

- Interrupting in conversations
- Being judgmental about friends, decisions, and likes and dislikes
- Telling them how they should feel
- Ridiculing their faults and mistakes
- Always telling them what they need to do
- Expecting unreasonable tasks beyond child's ability
- Being critical in spirit and arrogant in confrontation
- Showing conditional love
- Not explaining why some decisions are made
- Demanding perfection and never being satisfied
- Jumping to conclusions with misuse of your imagination

respond to authority very well, and my attempts to enforce my authority only hurt our relationship. She digs in her heels, and when it comes to a fight, she won't budge.

Sound familiar? Hey, if you ever feel like you're in a great position of authority, come try to tell Toy what to do; she'll put you in your place quickly. My show of authority to her is interpreted as nothing more than a four legged friend being picked on and bullied by a two-legged authoritarian (with a mustache).

Here's what I've further learned in my interactions with Toy. If I can get her to think that she wants to do something, and I spend some time enticing, entreating, and encouraging her positively, she'll allow me to walk beside her, and all I have to then do is guide her on her path. See the connection I'm making here?

I play the "relationship card" with the teens I meet with all the time. I'll say, "I'm not asking you to go this way because I'm your authority. I'm asking you to go this way because I want good things for you. I want you to end up in a place where you want to be, not where you don't want to be." I still have the "authority card" in my hand, but I choose to play the "relationship card" because it trumps everything on the table. My authority is shown on the face of that relationship card by the wisdom I bring, the opportunities I provide, the decisions I help them make, and the boundaries I set for them. It's an authority that is won, not demanded; and it is offered, not forced.

People change because of relationship, not authority.

JUDGING BUILDS WALLS

Many times, the good message that parents express to their kids is interpreted as judgment. Their intentions are good, but their timing is off because their understanding of what their children are living through is limited. Well-intended parents sometimes create dividing walls between their family relationships rather than bridges that connect them with their children.

Unfortunately, the good message of parenting often gets lost in translation of intent. The friction in relationships caused by what is said versus what is actually heard many times ignites a war of words and lights a fuse to an explosive attitude that detonates and destroys the delivery of much-needed messages of wisdom, scriptural insight, and ethical discussion.

When parents fail in their attempts to understand what is really happening in their children's lives, the timing of their well-intentioned comments often leaves children feeling judged.

The second area where many parents miss the opportunity for greatness in the lives of their children is when they fail to understand the diversity of the peer relationships their children are developing. Chances are, most kids have a racially diverse group of friends and a variety of relationships with acquaintances that will cause them to question what they've been taught in the process of developing their own belief systems. Kids are exposed to other religions and may even develop friendships with those of different faiths, causing them to question who's right and who's wrong. Many will get to know kids who are homosexual or have a wide range of acceptable behaviors, and they'll wonder where these friends fit into the lessons they've been taught. Others will wander through issues of alcohol, tobacco, definition of marriage, sanctity of life, divorce, sexual boundaries, and politically dividing promotions that call into question many of the life truths they have been raised to believe.

Truth with judgment pushes kids away; truth with relationship draws them to you.

It's important for parents to understand that perfection is impossible, authority can no longer be forced, and judging builds walls.

If teens experience all three of these components, it's easy to understand some of the behavior we see in kids. Think about it for a moment. If children *perceive* that parents are pushing perfection, *feel* life is more about exercise of authority than the pursuit of relationship, and *sense* judgment when they express themselves, it's no wonder that many kids want to be somewhere else physically, emotionally, and maybe even spiritually.

FOCUS EXERCISES

▌ KEY CONCEPTS

1. Kids sometimes interpret parents' *encouragement,* their holding to morals and biblical principles, and sharing of wisdom as being *critical.*

2. Your kids might think that you are *perfect.* They are beginning to learn that they are *not perfect.*

3. At times, *imperfect people* have a tough time being with *perfect people.*

4. Many teens come home after school *emotionally spent* and then interpret their parents' well-intended comments of encouragement and direction as a *demand for perfection.*

5. Because the culture has influenced a child's *view of authority,* a parent's show of authority *doesn't work as well* as it used to.

6. People don't change because of the *show of authority;* they change because of *relationship.* Similarly, consequences *teach lessons;* relationships *change the heart.*

7. What is *said,* and what is *heard,* are sometimes two different things.

8. Truth with *judgment* pushes kids away; truth with *relationship* draws them to you.

9. When children process the principles they have learned and begin to apply these to their culture, it is better for parents to walk *with them* in their journey than make them *avoid* the path parents desire them to follow.

What I wish parents knew about kids who think their parents are judgmental:

- Sometimes a child just needs to think out loud to process and have someone listen without giving an opinion.

- Not every teachable moment needs to become a time of teaching.

- Asking, "Are you asking me a question or wanting my opinion?" is a wonderful way to respect the kids and offer help rather than shove your opinion down their throats through lecture.

- Teaching your kids well doesn't mean you have to keep reminding them where they've blown it; they already know.

- Parents don't have to point out every way their kids can do things better.

- Despite a dad's good intentions, he might be missing the heart of his kids, who long to have a relationship with him.

- Mom's judgmental comments about controversial issues could move her kids to ignore all the wisdom she shares in other conversations.

- In parents' hearts, they feel like they are fulfilling their parenting role; but in their kids' hearts, they might be perceived to be extremely judgmental people to be avoided.

QUESTIONS FOR DISCUSSION

1. If every time you encountered a particular person, that person always corrected you, never quit telling you what you were doing wrong, and always had a better way of accomplishing your task, wouldn't you avoid that person?

2. Do you think that your kids think you want perfection displayed in their lives?

3. Are you hesitant to share your imperfections with your teens out of embarrassment or because you're fearful they'll know you aren't as perfect as they perceive you to be?

4. Are you driven to always correct your child and make sure there's a lesson behind every correction? If so, what do you think fuels that desire?

5. Do you think that sharing your imperfections with your teen can bring a sense of hope into his or her life?

6. Do you get frustrated that your kids don't respect the person you are or the position you hold in their lives?

7. Do you feel that you are "an authority" in the life of your children or have to "play your authority card" at times to get their attention and remind them of "who's the boss"?

8. Do you believe that the power of relationship has more of a chance of changing a child's heart than forcing your position of authority on him or her?

9. Do you think there are ways to teach moral and biblical values and help a child learn the difference between right and wrong without being judgmental?

10. Do you think that the position of perfection, authority, and judge can be interpreted as arrogance?

11. Do you have a tough time trusting your children because you know that they aren't perfect? Do your children have a tough time trusting you because they think you are perfect?

12. If a teen believes that church is the place you go to show off your perfection, what would be some ways that a parent could counter such
thinking?

ACTION POINT FOR THE WEEK

When you have a quiet moment with your kids, try to share some of your
imperfections. You'll be amazed how kids respond. They just might begin
to see you as "normal" and start to understand that it's okay to make mistakes, because we all make them. Your admission of imperfection conveys
a message that counters their feeling that you are demanding perfection
(remember, it's what they perceive), affirms your love for them "in their imperfections," and gives them hope that imperfection is pretty normal.

And if you don't think that these issues of perfection, authority, and
judgment are pertinent for you and your child, ask your teen these questions:

- Do you think that I want perfection from you?

- Do you think that I push my authority on you?

- Do you think that I'm a judgmental person?

Session
4

A NEW MODEL FOR PARENTING TEENS

I'm convinced that parenting kids is more than just an exercise in entertainment, improvement, and survival. Surely it's more than just making sure your sons don't look at porn and your daughters are virgins when they get married. And it's more than just the fulfillment of the challenge to move them from dependence to independence. I know the purpose of parenting is more than a boot camp of preparation for the wars they'll face in life. And parenting your kids is more than just fulfilling an obligation to "train up a child" so they can train up their children, and so on. Parenting kids is about relationships.

Remember, teens change because of relationship, not authority. They flourish in an atmosphere where they know that they have the freedom to make choices, are not shamed when they make mistakes, and are loved the most when they deserve it the least. So learning a few easy techniques to enhance your relationship with your child will create an arena for relationships that is critical to the new model of parenting teens.

YOUR UNIQUE ROLE AS A PARENT

Out of all the billions of people on this planet, God chose you to parent your child. This is true whether he or she is your birth child, your adopted child, a grandchild who has come into your life, or one of the kids in your neighborhood. God has crossed your life with theirs for reasons beyond what any parent will ever know. That means you have unique insights, wisdom, talents, skills, and values to give your child. In a culture that offers excitement, attraction, and promises of entertainment, it's easy for parents to feel that they can't compete. But kids really do want more than glitz and glamour. As human beings created in God's image, we are hardwired to want things with intrinsic value; your teens are no different.

The landscape of adolescence is forever changing.

Dads, chances are you're going to be the man in your daughter's life until you give her away to the man with whom she'll spend the rest of her life. Your involvement with her will shape her ideals about relationships with men and more than likely determine the types of interactions she has with others. While moms usually instill a sense of value into the life of a child, dads validate their existence. Leave or ignore your daughter and when she is old, she will still remember the scars from your lack of participation in her life.

And I'll just bet, Mom, that your relationship with your son will determine the type of woman he marries one day. You'll have the opportunity to help him become the man someone wants to share her life with. Because of you, he'll know compassion and empathy and develop sensitivity beyond what his manliness allows. Have a good relationship with him, and he will bring you years of blessings—for you will always be on his mind and in his heart until his dying day. Spend time correcting or ridiculing him, or do everything for him, and you'll force him to express his manhood unhealthily and never be happy with who he is as a man.

Dads, your relationship with your son is essential and a key influence in his development into a man of character. Withhold your blessing or your expression of approval for who he is and is to become, and the damage will be evident throughout his life. The message that he is your son with whom you are well pleased can usher into his life a world of contentment, and its suppression can haunt a man all the days of his life. Take care to ensure that he knows of your love for him. Make sure that of all the losses your son will experience in his life, you are not one of them.

Moms, you will teach your daughters how to love a man, how to love children, and how to balance many things in life. Your service is contagious, your diplomacy is elegant, and your hospitality shows grace in action beyond measure. Your daughter needs you, your thoughts, and your support. She does not need your nagging, shaming, or dominance. Your role is to help her become her own woman.

Here are some of the lessons I've learned over the years that I've found to be true in parenting teens:

- A discipline problem is usually a relationship problem.
- A communication problem is often rooted in relationship issues.
- The lack of understanding between a parent and child is usually the result of a few cracks in the relationship foundation.
- Kids change through relationship, not from the exercise of authority.
- Small issues become big issues where there is no relationship.
- Conflict becomes an enemy between two people when a relationship is no longer present, and conflicts are quickly resolved where relationships flourish.
- Lessons to be learned from each other are better taught when a bridge of relationship is formed between two people.
- Rules in your home not connected in relationship usually cause rebellion.
- A person best recognizes wisdom when there is a relationship.

And grandparents, what's your role in the life of your grandkids? The fun one! You get to eliminate all the stuff that didn't work with your kids and spend your time giving wisdom, love, and acceptance in a way that can't be felt from parents. Your grandkids desperately need you in their lives. You have the chance to take advantage of your wealth, knowledge, time, and position to add flavor to their lives. Do so to acknowledge their worth and to affirm the role that your kids are having in their lives.

Teens were created as relational beings, not herd animals. They long to connect, to engage with one another, and to have meaningful relationships. When personal connections don't happen, social molding, the impartation of wisdom, and the validation of value and self-esteem instilled by parents don't happen. But what does happen is this—new doors of opportunity open for parents to walk into the lives of their children. Those "Leave me alone!" signs hanging on their doors transform into welcome mats for those parents who have spent time developing relationships with their children.

Teaching in their early years, training in their adolescence years.

COMMIT TO SPENDING TIME WITH YOUR KIDS

So here's what I suggest to every family I come into contact with: find a place in your schedule so that you can get with your child once a week, one-on-one. Make it over a breakfast, an afternoon meeting over coffee, or a special designated dinner that you can have consistently and systematically. Begin doing this when your child turns thirteen and let him or her know of your commitment to get together every seven days just to spend time together. It's better to start early with this tradition. Waiting to meet with your kids when there's conflict is like trying to string communication lines in the middle of a hurricane. Build those avenues now, when the "weather" is quiet, and build them in a way that they'll survive any storm that comes into your family.

ASK QUESTIONS TO CREATE CONNECTIONS

When you get together, commit to not sharing your opinion unless asked, pledge (to yourself) not to correct language, thoughts, comments, or opinions, and be determined to get to know your child's way of thinking and personality over the next few years. For it is during this giving of your time that you can share wisdom, transfer a concept of value, share experiences, and provide the opportunity for a relationship to happen.

And when you do spend this time together, shift from a "teaching" mind-set to a "training" mentality. Consider that you've pretty much taught the material by the time your children reach their teen years, and now is the time to start training them to apply what you have built into their hearts.

Your questions will push them to pull up current and archived files and learn how to apply them to their lives. Your questions will convey a great sense of value to them. If you ask to get to know their hearts, and don't ask just as an entry point for you to share your opinion about something, they will eventually learn that this time is about them, and not about you.

Set aside a time every week to meet with your child.

As a matter of fact, when I meet with kids and spend time in a one-on-one setting, I choose to not share my opinion unless asked. This doesn't mean that I don't want to share it. There are times that I'm chompin' at the bit to give answers, share that deep insight that I have, or correct something they say that just doesn't fit. It's like putting together a jigsaw puzzle where I know where a particular piece "fits," but I let the person I'm putting the puzzle together with figure it out and come to an understanding of where it fits.

In due time, you will have an opportunity when your teens ask you a question. But wait for that question. When the question comes they are seeking wisdom or your insight. And they ask you because you have let them know that they are valued, they are worth your time, you care about them, and they feel a sense of comfort and trust in the atmosphere of discussion that you've created. Remember, training is helping them take what they already know and apply it to their lives. Your questions are just stirring their thinking to piece it all together to come to a conclusion.

If you feel like you're having a tough time asking questions and can't figure out how to kick-start the conversation, I've included a series of questions in the back of this book (Appendix A).

FOCUS EXERCISES

KEY CONCEPTS

1. Parenting kids is about a *relationship*.

2. Parents hold a unique position in their children's lives to offer *wisdom*, *relationship, time, value,* and *experience*.

3. You might be doing all the *right things* as a parent and yet not be what your *child needs* you to be.

4. Countering the effects of this culture won't happen by making sure *your child's room is clean* or *ensuring that she makes good grades*.

5. Parenting kids is more than just an exercise in *entertainment, improvement,* and *survival.*

6. Life lessons in the teen years are more *caught* than *taught.*

7. The purpose of asking questions is to get your children to take what they *already know* and learn how to *apply it* to their world. This *process of retrieval and application* is sometimes more important than the lesson to be learned.

8. A *fool* appears wise when he keeps his *mouth shut;* a *fool* delights in sharing his own *opinion* (Prov. 17:28).

9. Time is a *gift;* that's why it's called the *"present."*

QUESTIONS FOR DISCUSSION

1. Do you believe that your child, whether a preteen or teen, would really desire to have and maintain a relationship with you?

2. Other than the five items listed above (**wisdom, relationship, time, value,** and **experience**), what do you have to offer your child?

3. Knowing that one day in the future you might look back at this time and regret that you didn't spend more time with your child, do you think that there are items in your schedule that keep you from finding two hours a week when you can meet with your child?

4. Seriously, out of all the activities, offices, roles, pastimes, and commitments you have, where does your child rate in your list of priorities?

5. Do you spend time trying to give your child something that you didn't have? If so, then what's the true motivation behind your giving: to please your child or to please yourself?

6. Why is it so difficult to listen to your child's answers to your questions, when the answers they are giving are not necessarily what you would like to hear?

7. Are you uncomfortable spending time with your child when there is silence?

8. Do you think there is a difference in the way that girls and guys learn and have conversations? Why so?

9. If your dad or mom would have spent time with you like I'm encouraging you to spend time with your kids, do you think that your relationship would have been any different than it is now?

▌ ACTION POINT FOR THE WEEK

Ask your children if they would like to get together once a week for coffee, ice cream, a hamburger, a trip to different restaurants, a movie with a follow-up dessert discussion, breakfast, or a morning workout shadowed by a donut throw-down. Tell them that you hope that they will "just want to get together." That first time you do get together, have a list of questions you could ask should the atmosphere turn silent. And *don't* share your opinions, comments, criticisms, or corrections. See what happens, and remember you're creating an atmosphere for future times together. You don't have to do everything in one meeting.

Session
5

STOP CONTROLLING,
START TRUSTING

When your children, even beginning at age twelve, start to understand that you are *for them* making decisions, *for them* taking control of their lives, *for them* developing their independence, *for them* making good choices, and *for them* showing you how they can do it, you'll have kids who respond to your correction, input, wisdom, and relationship in a way that draws them to you.

— A TEEN'S LONGING FOR CONTROL —

When it comes to making choices in their lives, teens want three things. They want to make decisions about themselves. They want to feel like they're in control. And they want opportunities to prove their maturity and show parents that they can do it. Don't you want the same? You do because you want your children to make a good choice about a spouse. You want them to be able to choose which direction to take when confronted with alternatives. You want them to say no because it's a good decision, and not to say yes just to prove to you that they can make decisions for themselves.

You want your children to be in control enough to choose the right path when some young man wants to sleep with your daughter or when your son is offered the opportunity to smoke pot. You want your teens to take control of their own choices because you don't want to control them when they leave home.

Here's how some kids feel about parental control:

- "My parents and I were fighting, but for two different things. They were fighting for protection; I was fighting for control."

- "They wouldn't let me do anything and they would never give me a reason why . . . I kept thinking, 'I'm eighteen and they treat me like I'm twelve.'"

- "They never trust me to do anything, so I started to take control of my life behind their back."

- "I started smoking just to prove to my parents that it was one area of my life they didn't control. And when they grounded me for smoking, I felt good because I knew I was in control of my life."

- "I wanted to prove to my parents that they couldn't control me . . . I think that's why I tried to kill myself."

- "I felt alive when I was in control and everyone except my parents knew me as one who could be in control."

- "My parents are control freaks. They trust no one . . . They'll never trust me, so I quit listening to them long ago."

- "The tighter they clamped down, the more I wanted to fight back. Most of the problems I have in life are because of my parents. They didn't train me; they ruined me. All because they wanted to be in control."

Many times parents take control of their children's lives, or won't relinquish control as children get older, because they believe that without their involvement their kids will not be in control. And they take control in more ways than just limiting privileges or taking away objects of desire to show consequences for inappropriate behavior. Control of your child can be shown through threats, name-calling, blaming, ridicule, mind games, jealousy, sarcasm, manipulation, isolation, economics, domination, intimidation, and verbal and physical assaults. When parents exert control through these means, it's not hard to predict the outcome.

LETTING THEM LEARN TO MAKE CHOICES

Do you think your kids aren't ready to make their own choices? Of course they're not. The only way they will be ready is for you to give up control a little bit at a time, thus giving them control at the same pace so they can become ready. Don't force them to have to rebel to gain control of new territory that will eventually be theirs.

It's time to quit controlling, and start trusting. And you ask, "Trusting what?" Great question. First of all, trust that they're going to be teens. They'll be exposed to more and more with each passing year, will become curious about concepts they've never thought about before, will make some bad decisions, and will make some mistakes. Their immaturity will play out until they mature. It's a time for them to "find themselves," "push the limits," discover their sexuality, and start that path to independence where they can "do it themselves." It's all normal stuff. Trust me.

The transfer of control is important in letting a child grow up and start to develop.

Second, trust what you've taught them. The seeds that you've sown into their lives will one day come to fruition. And all those values, biblical principles, morals, good lessons, character traits, and respectful habits will rise to the top . . . one day. God promises that He will bring to completion that which he has started (Phil. 1:6). Trust Him.

Third, trust that God is involved in your child's life as well, even when you can't see it. He was involved in your child's life long before you were, and He'll be involved long after you're gone. Trust Him.

TRAINING THAT MOVES A CHILD TO INDEPENDENCE

I, too, wanted a better relationship with my kids than I had with my parents. And I wanted to give them things, maybe because I wanted to outdo what my parents did for me in hopes of trying to be a better parent. What

I found was that so much of what I thought I was doing for my kids, I was really doing for myself. I was getting something from the relationship, and I was getting value from having them be dependent on me. Somewhere along the line of raising kids, there must be a shift in a parenting style that quits providing everything for children and helps them learn to provide for themselves.

I'm not saying that you should quit giving your twelve-year-old gifts and money and make him or her head out to get a job, but I am saying that the move from total dependence to total independence should be in the forefront of all your actions as your child heads into the adolescent years.

I'm also not telling you that you should cut off your children at age eighteen and make them fend for themselves. But I am saying that an eighteen-year-old would be better off having a concept that you are not obligated to provide for him and you owe him nothing . . . and want to give him everything. This mind-set forces a desire on his part to begin to develop skills that will allow him to make the transition into successful adulthood and puts you in a position of offering and helping, rather than giving him a sense of entitlement. The mind-set is far better adapted to a parenting style when a child is headed into junior high school than deciding to give your child a quick crash course on "How to Be Independent in Six Months" right after he turns eighteen.

So quit focusing on pleasing, protecting, and providing for your child, and shift your focus to preparing your child to leave home and not be dependent on you! Kids have a natural desire to be dependent on their parents as long as the parents provide. Provision quickly moves to enabling if your actions don't wean them from their dependence upon you as years pass.

Training is taking what your child knows and applying it to the world they live in.

The following terms have become common for kids who "fail to launch" in their post-teen years:

- A *boomerang kid* comes back home because he can't function in the world he is to live in.

- A *twentysomething* is caught in waithood, waiting for adulthood to happen.

- A *parasite single* sucks the life from Mom and Dad because she just doesn't want to be independent.

- A *twixter* (one caught betwixt adolescence and adulthood) justifies his existence by blaming it on the economy, on politics, or on social influences.

- Young men and women caught in *emerging adulthood* complain of having a *quarter-life crisis,* so they become NEETs—Not in Education, Employment, or Training.

- In Japan, these kids are called *freeters,* and in Mexico and Spain they're called ni-ni— "neither study, nor work" (ni estudia, ni trabaja).

What are you doing for your kids that they can pick up and start doing for themselves—not because you don't want to continue to help your child do these things, but because you need to let them start doing some things to help usher in the new years of fostering independence?

Here are some things you can require from your children when they turn thirteen:

- Getting themselves out of bed with an alarm clock

- Picking out their own clothes every morning

- Getting ready for school and eating breakfast

- Getting to school on time

- Doing their own laundry

- Cleaning their own rooms (even if you have a housekeeper)

- Doing their homework without you having to nag them to do it
- Making their own snacks after school

The point of the exercise is not taking away from your parenting role but changing your child-rearing role to now encompass training to help your children learn to begin to take care of themselves. It's not less parenting; it's a different type of parenting.

TRAINING GOALS FOR YOUR TEEN

Here are some other training focus points you might want to consider:

- Handling finances
- Making good decisions
- Breaking the mind-set of entitlement
- Keeping relationships when there's conflict
- Handling stress and resolving disagreements
- Not always having to be right
- What to do when you're wrong
- Treating a friend with kindness
- Finding the right spouse
- The value of a good day's work
- Setting objectives and working toward those goals
- Standing for what you believe
- Essentials of a disciplined life
- Integrity and keeping your word
- The need for community and the development of relationships
- Having fun and learning how to take care of yourself

- How to surround yourself with wise people

- Finding the job that fits your skill set

- Making money and living within your means

- Changing a tire on a car

- How to ask for help

TEACHING TEENS "I OWE YOU NOTHING. BUT I WANT TO GIVE YOU EVERYTHING."

You must break the entitlement mentality that has become a cultural influence. I would let teens know the following: "I owe you nothing, but I want to give you everything." When your children begin to see you as one who is giving because you want to, as one who will help them learn new ways of living with a goal of independence, and as one who is always thinking ahead, their response to you will be one of gratitude and respect.

OFFER FREEDOM TO MAKE MISTAKES

You can keep your children from making mistakes in any of the following ways:

- Don't let them do anything or participate with anyone in any activity.

- Do everything for them so they never have opportunity to make a decision.

- Don't teach about making decisions in life.

Give your children the opportunity to make mistakes, coupled with the freedom to make mistakes without the fear of shame, ridicule, or sarcasm. This gives them permission to exercise their decision-making muscle so that they can carry the heavier loads of adulthood they will be required to lift.

— TRANSFERRING RESPONSIBILITY TO YOUR CHILD —

Under the banner of "overprotection" many parents isolate their kids, deny them the opportunity to fail, suppress their teens' desire to make decisions, beat down their spirit if they make a mistake, and withhold opportunities of learning that can turn good kids into disobedient kids.

Trust what you've taught your kids.

I'm not saying that parents should irresponsibly expose their kids to everything and let the world teach them through the school of hard knocks with the mentality of "fend for yourself." We don't throw our children into the deep end of the pool and yell, "Swim!" to teach them to keep their head above water. We start in the shallow end and gradually let them go farther as they show that they can do better. Will they go under at times? Yes. Will they swallow water and choke? Yes. Will they go too far sometimes? Yes. I teach kids to swim this way because I know that they'll one day be in that deep end. I can always be on the watch . . . and I can jump in with them if they need my help. But I've got to let them learn to swim in their own pool, and give them the opportunity to utilize the skills that I have taught them, so they won't go under when I'm not around to ensure their safety. I also stress the importance of practice, practice, practice.

When your tween begins turning into a teen, start flavoring your conversations with comments and questions that transfer you making decisions and placing that responsibility on them. You can say things like:

- "It's your choice."

- "Where do you want to eat tonight?"

- "What do you want?"

- "You decide."

4. Somewhere along the line of raising kids, there must be a shift in a *parenting style* that *quits providing* everything for children and helps them learn to *provide for themselves.*

5. Helping a child understand that you *owe him nothing* but want to *give him everything* helps break the mind-set of entitlement.

6. You can keep teens from *making mistakes* by not letting them *participate* in anything or with anyone, do *everything* for them so they never have to make a decision, and *don't train* them about needing to make good decisions.

7. Under the banner of *overprotection* many parents *isolate* their kids, *deny* them the opportunity to fail, *suppress* their teens' desire to make decisions, beat down their spirit if they make a mistake, and *withhold* opportunities of learning that can turn good kids into disobedient kids.

Trust that God is involved in the life of your child.

8. *Practice, practice, practice* teaches a teen the difference between right and wrong.

9. *Provision* quickly moves to *enabling* if your actions don't wean them from their *dependence upon* you as years pass.

10. You don't have to *shame* them when they already know they made a *mistake.*

QUESTIONS FOR DISCUSSION

1. What do you think is your motivation for doing as much as you do for your child?

2. Do you do more for your children than your parents did for you?

3. Would your teens welcome the opportunity to start making more decisions for themselves?

4. Are you moving your child to be more and more independent as the years pass?

5. What would it mean for your child to make a mistake, or make a poor decision?

6. Do you perceive your child's mistakes as a reflection on your parenting ability, or do you just chalk it up to experience?

7. Do your kids feel like you owe them everything? Are they consumed with a spirit of entitlement? And if so, who's created that atmosphere?

8. Would your kids define you as a permissive parent or one who is overly protective?

9. At the current pace of helping your children become independent and able to make life-changing decisions, will they be ready to function on their own by the time they turn eighteen?

10. What message do you give your kids in your response to their mistakes?

▮ ACTION POINT FOR THE WEEK

This week, give your child, no matter what age, one more responsibility than he or she had last week, not with the intent of lightening your load but of giving the opportunity for your child, whether a tween or a teen, to make more decisions.

ADD CLEAR BOUNDARIES

The mark of a good parent is not necessarily a well-behaved child. And a good kid isn't always one who never gets into trouble, makes a bad decision, or fails a class. I've observed that a mark of good parenting is determined by not only the way a child acts at home during his or her teen years, but also how a child engages and lives in later years.

Sometimes I've seen that the healthiest person in a whole family can be one who was often viewed as rebellious as a teen. Your teens might be rebelling because they really want some structure in your home, where they know the expectations and understand the boundaries and privileges. They want to know what the limits are and where the fences are in their lives and your home, and they want the freedom and the opportunity to operate within those boundaries.

I've watched kids behave wonderfully at home but then had them share with me how much they hate their parents, can't wait to get away from them, and never want to see them again when they eventually leave their house. I've seen kids so isolated from the real world and so controlled by parents that they behave well in their younger years but are complete messes once they are out on their own. I've seen fear in the eyes of well-behaved kids when their parents approach, and it doesn't take a rocket scientist to figure out what's really going on back at the ranch. On two tragic occasions,

I've heard news that a child committed suicide, and upon hearing the news I was saddened yet not surprised because of what I had observed.

What's the common denominator in all these situations? Parents who are much too controlling because they don't have a plan in place or a structure in order that permits them, as parents, to not have to be in control. When parents don't have mutually and fully understood boundaries within their home, they are forced to be strict, which only adds to a teen's or preteen's frustration. We'll talk about this a little more in the next chapter.

The most important shift that must happen is the defining of what discipline is for your home as your child ages into his or her adolescent years.

During the preteen years, so much of discipline is focused on keeping children out of trouble, while teaching them the values of respect, obedience, honesty, and how to function in their world. Consequences are seen as more of a punishment for violating what Mom and Dad desire for their child. Now, that all begins to shift.

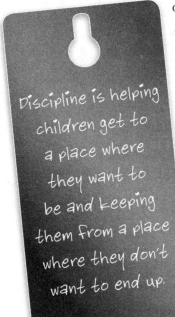

Discipline is helping children get to a place where they want to be and keeping them from a place where they don't want to end up.

When your children enter their teen years, the definition of discipline changes as well. That new definition is this: discipline's goal is to help teens get to where they want to be and keep them from a place they don't want to end up. It's now applied in an ordered system of boundaries, rules, and consequences in a relational setting that focuses on allowing them to begin becoming responsible adults. It's all about them.

So when you're structuring your home and lining out those boundaries that allow your children to begin to take control of their lives, be sure to keep in mind that this system is indeed about the way you operate your home, but the focus should be on them with an understanding that you want them to not only understand where the "fences" are, but you desire for them to make decisions, choose wisely, treat people with respect, and begin to understand they have as much to do with their future as you do as their parent.

DEVELOPING EFFECTIVE TECHNIQUES FOR PARENTING TEENS

I've found that setting clear boundaries, developing rules that uphold what I believe, administering agreed-upon consequences for inappropriate behavior, and then allowing kids the freedom to make choices within the boundaries provides an opportunity for me to back down on the strictness and focus more on the relationship. This model gives teens freedom, the ability to make choices and control their lives to some degree, and it forces them to assume responsibility for their lives. It also takes me out of the role of authoritarian and puts me into a role of relationship. As I've said many times, kids change because of relationship, not authority.

Structure gives freedom and opportunity.

DEVELOPING A BELIEF SYSTEM OF RULES AND CONSEQUENCES FOR YOUR HOME

Next, set the rules for your home for behaviors (and probable behaviors) that are particular to your home for your situation and for the specific issues you're dealing with. Limit your long list of rules to the ten most important for your family. These need to be determined by age, your history with a particular child, what you believe, and what values you determine are important for your family.

Here's my list of ten things that I think are important enough to develop rules around, letting everyone know what the family policy is on these particular items and what the consequence will be for violating a family rule.

1. Bullying
2. Disrespect
3. Dishonesty
4. Drugs/alcohol
5. Disobedience
6. Failing classes
7. Inappropriate Internet activity
8. Sexual activity
9. Texting while driving (Parents better not do this!)
10. Deceitfulness and lying

List the ten most important things to develop rules around for your home:

1. _____
2. _____
3. _____
4. _____
5. _____
6. _____
7. _____
8. _____
9. _____
10. _____

Next, determine the consequences for breaking the rules. This is basically a system that says, "You do the crime, you do the time." And don't rescue your child from the consequences. The value of determining boundaries within your family, and then setting rules and consequences, is to let this model be the authority so that you don't have to parent with strictness. Once this system is in place, then you will have the opportunity to develop deeper relationships with your kids.

So what consequences do you set? To formulate what consequence goes with each rule, determine what your children like doing the most, and take that away when they violate the most important rule that you have established.

List ten things your child likes:

1. _____

2. _____

3. _____

4. _____

5. _____

6. _____

7. _____

8. _____

9. _____

10. _____

> Rules without relationship creates rebellion; relationship without rules causes chaos.

Decide what the consequence will be for each of your rules and list them below.

RULE	CONSEQUENCE
1. _____	_____
2. _____	_____
3. _____	_____
4. _____	_____
5. _____	_____
6. _____	_____
7. _____	_____
8. _____	_____
9. _____	_____
10. _____	_____

Now, let the system work. Loosen up a little, and trust what you have put together. And don't rescue your kids from the consequences of their behavior; they'll only have to learn that lost lesson at the next juncture of conflict from inappropriate behavior. Here's an example: if your child is disrespectful, and you've all agreed that disrespect in the home means that he'll lose use of a cell phone for a week, then make sure that he loses it for a week, in hopes of your child learning a lesson that disrespect doesn't get him to a good place. If you rescue your child from that consequence, he'll only have to learn that lesson the next time he's disrespectful.

FOCUS EXERCISES

KEY CONCEPTS

1. Discipline can be defined as an effort to help teens get to *where they want to be* and keep them from a place they *don't want to end up*.

2. Setting clear *boundaries*, developing *rules* that uphold what you believe, administering agreed-upon *consequences* for inappropriate behavior, and then allowing kids the *freedom to make choices* within the boundaries creates a model where relationships can flourish.

3. Kids change because of *relationship*, not *authority*.

4. While conflict can be healthy and promote growth, *constant conflict* can drown relationships.

5. Limit your long list of rules to the *ten most important* for your family.

6. The value of *determining boundaries* within your family, and then *setting rules and consequences*, is to let this model be the authority so that you don't have to parent with *strictness*.

7. Your child's *understanding of* and *agreement to* the rules you collectively set forth in your home will help her understand that consequences are of *her choosing,* not a *parent's* choosing.

8. The *purpose of consequences* is to get your child to *think* about those consequences the next time he or she wants to *repeat* the inappropriate behavior. This will help him make better *future* choices.

QUESTIONS FOR DISCUSSION

1. Why is it hard to set rules in your home?

2. Will it be a challenge to get your kids to agree to the consequences for the violation of rules that you set in your home?

3. What are the five things that you would like to see different in your home?

4. Do you find yourself constantly rescuing your child from consequences of inappropriate behavior? If so, what do you think your motivation is for feeling you have to rescue him or her?

5. Do you feel that allowing your children to suffer the consequences of their behavior will hurt your relationship with them?

6. Do you feel that you will experience a sense of relief when rules and consequences are set up at your home, or that it will only be another burden for you to enforce?

7. Do you believe that determining rules and consequences will be met with anger or met with relief?

ACTION POINT FOR THE WEEK

List a few things that you would like to see changed in your home; either because your current mode of operation is no longer effective or because you'd like to see some things handled differently to produce some different results. When you're sitting down for a meal this week with your family, ask this: "Guys, I'd like to see a few changes in the following areas . . . what do you think?" Then list those areas (for example, respect in the house, cleanliness, curfews, giving them more responsibility, helping them attain greater independence) and just wait for their responses.

If each time you eat with your family you come to the table with a question you want to ask, everyone will anticipate that question and adapt to being ready to answer and discuss your topic. Give it time. People want to be heard, they want others to listen, and all kids are dying to talk or learn how to put words to their feelings.

SUBTRACT STRICTNESS

When parents are strict and in control, many kids are well behaved yet feel a deep contempt for their parents. And if provoked enough through limitations, isolation, authoritarian discipline, and exasperating sternness, teenage angst can quickly turn to intentional disobedience and focused disrespect. Many kids will eventually express their anger of not getting what they want by violating everything a parent has taught or desires for them, just to show Mom and Dad who is really in control.

If parents don't give opportunity for their teens to flex and exercise their decision-making muscle, and make them feel like they're in control of their lives, many teens will fight for that opportunity. I've seen many teens who want control, want independence, want to make decisions, want some more freedom, and want to mature—all great longings for a teen. When parents keep that from happening because of their strictness, a teen's fight might just be rooted in a good cause. Remember that scripture about parents not provoking a child to wrath? Parents, is your strictness forcing your children to have to fight for their freedom? It's a question that all parents should ask of themselves when encountering what is thought to be rebellious behavior.

Now, I'm not saying that parents shouldn't be strict. I'm encouraging parents to not be as strict as children begin to enter their adolescent years. Everything in your children's lives begins to change when they enter their tween years. They begin to think more abstractly than concretely. Hormones begin their natural process. They are enlightened to a new world that they never knew existed: one filled with rejection, hatred, hurt, pain, difficulty, struggle, and conflict. Their desire to explore curious thinking moves beyond the confines of your home and now embraces an exciting world that they want to experience. And what you will find is that your parenting styles have to shift as well. Discussions need to replace all those lectures. Silence ushers in the opportunity for your children to think more and be told what to do less. Teaching transforms into training.

We have to give our kids the opportunity to make decisions.

The model of teaching switches to a model of training: helping teens take what they have learned and apply it to the world where they are living. Because of this switch, parents must be willing to make a switch in their rigidity, control, dominating approach, and inflexibility.

Lightening up on your approach isn't an indicator that what "was important" is "no longer important." It's quite the opposite. You must ease up on your involvement so that your child can embrace the need for his involvement in his life and destiny. Throttling back on your intensity to ensure a child learns a lesson gives your child the chance to internalize this much-needed lesson and learn the value of its application. And we all know that lessons have a way of "sticking" in a child's life when he or she is the one who is learning, as opposed to our being the ones who are teaching.

DETERMINING PRIVILEGES AND EXPECTATIONS

Here are some areas of privileges and beliefs that are the most asked-about topics at my speaking engagements. This is not an exhaustive list:

- Cell phone usage and texting
- Church attendance
- Curfew on weekdays and weeknights

- Dating or courting
- Dress and appearance
- Driving a car
- Extracurricular activities
- Social media activity
- Going to the mall
- Doing homework
- Internet access
- Involvement in activities
- Movies to watch
- Music
- Rewards for positive behavior
- Sleepovers
- Employment

I'll bet you can come up with other items that need to be tackled in your home. List your top twenty privileges:

1. _____
2. _____
3. _____
4. _____
5. _____
6. _____
7. _____
8. _____
9. _____
10. _____
11. _____
12. _____
13. _____
14. _____
15. _____

Don't be so strict; your kids can handle it.

16. _____

17. _____

18. _____

19. _____

20. _____

After listing all those areas that you think need addressing, go through each one and determine a timeline that would let your children know year-by-year expectations for them that show them how you desire to move them to independence and allow them to make more and more choices about their lives as they get older.

— A STRATEGY FOR PRIVILEGES THAT WORKS —

When trying to figure out the schedule of what privileges to give when, I would encourage you to consider this: I've come to the conclusion that many parents could avoid a lot of drama if they would just give what their kids will eventually get anyway, just a bit sooner. If you think your child should get a cell phone at age fifteen, give it to her at fourteen and a half. If you don't think he should choose his clothing until age sixteen, let him start at fifteen and a half. Giving privileges to your kids a few months early maintains a relationship that could be destroyed if they have to rebel for their freedom. Look, you're eventually going to give the privilege to your child anyway. So give the privilege, build some agreed parameters around it, and take it away should he fail to hold up his end of the agreement. Use the space below to create your timeline for transferring control of each privilege to your child:

Sometimes parents protect their kids a little bit too long.

PRIVILEGE

TIMELINE WITH MILESTONES

1.
2.
3.
4.
5.
6.
7.
8.
9.
10.
11.
12.
13.
14.
15.
16.
17.
18.
19.
20.

—— LEARNING TO PICK YOUR BATTLES WISELY ——

While conflict can be healthy and promote growth, *constant* conflict can drown relationships. Parents who engage in a battle over every little thing they disagree with in their teens' lives—from unmade beds to a poor test grade—will find that the only changes they get from their teens are increasing tides of resentment washing over every member of the family. It's essential to the life of the family and the sanity of each member for parents to identify the important battles that need to be fought and leave the less important ones to take care of themselves.

PICKING FIVE THINGS YOU WOULD LIKE TO —— SEE CHANGED IN YOUR HOME ——

If you had to limit confrontation of issues at your home to just five things, what would those five areas of confrontation be? Pick your battles wisely; you only have five.

Would it be a scuffle to limit or restrict the music they listen to? Would it be a melee over their hair—how they wear it, what color it is, the length, or them shaving their head? Would it be the battle over going to church or choosing which church to go to? Would there be a war over their academics and grades and performance, or would it be the types of peers they want to hang out with? Would it be a skirmish over the amount of time they spend playing video games or disputes over how much time a teen needs to spend online?

Would there be a conflict over your definition and their definition of modesty—whether your daughter is showing too much cleavage or your son has his pants hanging halfway down his rear end? Would you choose to have encounters about the kids having tattoos and getting piercings, or would there be arguments over the type of makeup your kids wear? Could there be fracases over social media language, whether it is what your child writes or the wording and comments of some of their friends' posts? Would you struggle over the use of words that suddenly seem more present and appropriate than words of yesteryear?

Would there be frays about relationships you've cautioned your child to remain distant from? Would you fight over the issues of disobedience, disrespect, and dishonesty? Or would you put up your dukes over the types of movies your child watches? Would it be worth dueling over whether your child could be sexually active or challenging a child's desire to use alcohol and drugs? Would there be a kerfuffle when a child doesn't keep his or her room tidy and clean? Would there be controversies over a child drinking and driving, or clashes over your child texting while driving?

Let me tell you why I think this topic of picking your battles wisely is so important. I believe that kids are overwhelmed in a culture that bombards them with information, new lifestyles, new challenges, and new pressures to perform and appear certain ways. That increased pressure is moving our teens from normal teenage angst (apprehension or insecurity) to increasing levels of anxiety (an overwhelming uneasiness and apprehension about future uncertainties) and depression.

The last thing any parent wants to do is to push his or her child beyond the normal limits of teenage angst, in the name of integrity, principle, and high standards, only to find out through some tragedy or storm blowing through his or her neck of the woods what is really important.

WHAT'S IMPORTANT AND WHAT'S NOT

Do I feel that the battles I've listed are unimportant? No! It's just that I believe in many situations there are battles that can wait to be fought, there are some that can be lost that won't change the bigger picture effort of the war, and there are some that are worth dying for. The question I ask parents frequently is, "Are you willing to die on that hill?" When they share various impasses they're having with a child when it comes to privileges, rules, boundaries, and correctional comments, I want them to think through their battle plan.

FOCUS EXERCISES

KEY CONCEPTS

1. Many kids will eventually *express their anger* over not getting what they want by *violating* everything a parent has taught or desires for them, just to show Mom and Dad who is really in *control*.

2. Many parents could avoid a lot of *drama* if they would just give their kids what they will eventually get anyway, just a bit *sooner*.

3. Pick your *battles* wisely.

4. There are battles that *can wait* to be fought, there are some that *can be lost* that won't change the bigger picture effort of the war, and there are some that are *worth dying* for.

5. When determining current and future privileges, it is helpful to put those privileges on a *timeline*, which gives some *future perspective* to the privileges you allow *today*.

6. While conflict can be *healthy* and *promote growth*, *constant* conflict can *drown* relationships.

7. The last thing any parent wants to do is to push his or her child beyond the normal limits of *teenage angst*, in the name *of integrity, principle, and high standards*.

QUESTIONS FOR DISCUSSION

1. Out of all the hills out there on the landscape of adolescence, which ones are you willing to die on?

2. What issues can be allowed to simmer on the back burner while you move that which needs to be cooked to the front burner?

3. What are the major issues for your family, and what are the minor issues that can be dealt with later?

4. What current issues will die out on their own, and which ones demand your attention?

5. What character traits for your kids need to be learned now, and what can be learned later?

6. What are the five things that you would like to see different in your home?

7. With the backdrop of teen suicides on the increase in a culture that your teen strives to survive in, is it really that important to mainly focus all your efforts on the cleanliness and tidiness of his or her room?

8. Which do you think is more important—the relationship that you have with your child or having him or her follow all the rules?

ACTION POINT FOR THE WEEK

There's a lot of work to be done in this chapter. From determining privileges to strategizing on a timeline, from picking battles wisely to narrowing down your five choices of what you would like to see changed around your home, it's easy to get caught up in just putting together another To Do list to put up on the refrigerator, hoping that if everyone will just "follow the rules", all will be well in your home.

Don't forget to add the relationship component to your lists that you come up with. An easy way to include your kids in this process is to ask them questions at dinner to make sure that you have their input into these various tasks we're asking you to do.

- Ask them what they believe their greatest privileges are.

- Ask them what they think the various expectations should be in your home.

- Ask them what they think the areas needing to be tackled in your home are.

- Ask them what five things they would like to see changed in the home.

You might be surprised how engaged they are and how desirous they might be to see "change" happen in your home.

Session 8

SEE CONFLICT AS A PRECURSOR TO CHANGE

I've been counseling teens for years, and I always have to remind myself: *These are teens. There's going to be conflict. I'm here to help them grow deeper in their understanding. Our relationship must remain intact even if I get angered over not getting what I want for them.* I must enter the conflict with the teen by understanding that conflict is a precursor to change, and my focus must be not on what has happened (or is happening currently) but on what will come out of our resolution.

Conflict hurts. If one walks away from conflict feeling a sense of winning, then I'm sure that the other walks away hurt. And hurt, within the context of a family, affects every member. Winning is not the answer, but learning to love when you've been offended is. It's called grace: moving toward an offender who has violated your values, principles, and standards. And here's the hardest part: forgiving teens for what they have done to you, even if they don't admit it. This is a tough lesson, but one that allows families to grow deeper than they could ever have imagined.

USING CONFLICT TO CREATE
DEEPER RELATIONSHIPS

When the dashboard warning light of anger flashes on your control panel, it is a signal to you that something is wrong. You must overcome your fear of conflict wherever that fear comes from and understand that your role is to counter the negative influences in your child's life.

To ignore the potential for conflict and to disengage from your child when these lights come on only allows for future behaviors, habits, and pathways to be reckoned with at a later time. Avoid issues now, and they will come later when they are much bigger, when consequences are usually much greater.

> If you have teens, you are going to have conflict.

To embrace the conflict ushers in a world of change that has the possibility of keeping your child from having to walk a path he or she really never wants to be on. Confronting minor issues now saves you the energy of having to deal with bigger issues later.

Conflict will come if you have teens. This is the perfect opportunity to shift "teaching" into "training" and show your children how to use the skills and knowledge that have been built into them through the years. To miss the opportunity for conflict means that you miss the opportunity to grow your relationship to a level you've always wanted.

SCHEDULE A TIME TO WORK THROUGH CONFLICT

Call it your "Confrontation over Coffee" time, your "Coke and Conflict" time, or your "Disagreements During Donuts" time, but find a time to sit down and let your child know, no matter what age he or she is, that this is the place, the opportunity, and the time to resolve any issues that arise. I always like having these types of talks in a public setting as I'm not walking on anyone's turf, and having others present has a way of keeping emotions in check should they begin to inflate.

When comments like these go through your head, chances are they are a dashboard warning sign of potential conflict:

- "I'm not comfortable about that."
- "I don't like the situation."
- "I don't feel good about my child's involvement in this."
- "I can't support this activity."
- "This makes me mad when he does this."
- "We need to think of a different course of action."
- "There's got to be an alternative."
- "This isn't good."
- "This isn't going to happen."
- "Is this what she really wants?"

UNDERSTANDING THE HIGH COST OF UNRESOLVED CONFLICT

What most people don't realize is that there is a great cost to unresolved conflict. All the time spent in the presence of unresolved conflict when relationships come to a standstill is time that could have been spent building a deeper relationship and helping your children make the changes they need in their teen years.

I know these things . . .

1. Teens are going to have conflict with parents.

2. The goal of conflict resolution has got to be about the person I'm having the conflict with.

3. I want to speak the truth in love.

Don't avoid conflict.

LOVING WHEN YOU DON'T FEEL LIKE IT

In more than three decades of living and working with kids, I've learned that if I walk away from the relationship every time someone offends me,

> *Your child will handle conflict in his life that is about to come in the same way you handle conflict with him now.*

then I allow that person's actions to determine the type of relationship I really want to have. I've been disappointed a lot. I've been offended many times by many kids. I've been disrespected and disobeyed, and have had many who have been dishonest with me. I've been taken advantage of, stolen from, and ridiculed. And while it hurts every time I feel the sting from their lack of consideration, I know that if I quit and give up, the relationship stops, and the hope for anything in the future becomes dim.

To love someone when you have been wronged is tough, but it's essential in communicating a love that is beyond your capability. It's a love that will win out if you don't quit. Even if you don't feel like it.

IT'S CALLED GRACE

For me, it's called grace. It's moving relationally toward a person when he or she has wronged you. It's opening the door of your heart when every part of you wants to shut it off. It's engaging when you have every right to disengage. It's offering help when someone's actions have violated everything you believe in, hope for, and want for that person. It's staying involved in the relationship when someone has violated your rules, ignored your advice, or hurt you through lies, deceit, and manipulation. When you feel good about giving grace, it probably isn't grace.

WHAT GRACE LOOKS LIKE IN A FAMILY

Here are some examples of what grace may look like with your child when your feelings are telling you otherwise:

- It's taking your child out to dinner when he's grounded for stealing money out of your purse.

- It's taking your daughter away for a couple of days to spend some quality time with her after you find out she's been having sex with her boyfriend.

- It's going up to your drama queen's room and sitting down and talking to her a few minutes after she blew up at your wife and used some words that you'll never find in Scripture.

- It's hugging your son and telling him, "We're going to get through this," after he tells you that his girlfriend is pregnant.

- It's not saying what you want to say (and have every reason to), and saying what needs to be heard when your tough guy just got expelled from school for defending the honor of his sister . . . the wrong way.

- It's taking your son to sit down for a man-to-man talk instead of wanting to poke his eyes out after your wife finds him looking at pornography on the Internet.

- It's not saying anything when a lot could be said, allowing the feelings of wrongdoing the opportunity to teach a lesson that your words could never achieve.

Grace is receiving something when you don't deserve it.

Your movement toward your children when they make mistakes, choose poorly, encounter problems, or violate your standards lets them know that the issues have more to do with them than they do with you. Your actions by remaining engaged help them keep focused on their responsibility for what they have done or what they will need to do. And it keeps you in the relational position of being one who wants to help them through their difficulties, rather than one who assumes responsibility to "fix" what has happened, solve the issue, or exert your authority.

It's a movement toward them when every part of you is crying out, "Walk away." It's tough, but well worth it in the long run of adolescence. It moves you from the authoritative directive style of their preteen years into a relational instructor mentality that sends a message that you will never leave them, you are for them, and you will be with them whatever they encounter in life. Talk about some teachable moments!

Please understand this: you can relate with your children well, ask a million questions, stop controlling everything in their lives, help them become independent, quit being so strict, learn that conflict is good as you pick your battles wisely, and spend all the time in the world with them. But if you retract your relationship when they mess up, you invalidate all you've been building, and all your good intentions of loving your child through their adolescent years will go down the drain.

GRACE AND LOVE TRUMP REBELLION AND PAIN

With head hung low, Bri responded, "Love me when I least deserve it, 'cause that's when I need it the most." Bri's answer stopped me dead in my tracks. As I hugged her, I kept thinking, *What she needs is grace.* Bri needed to be loved when she didn't deserve it . . . loved when I felt anything but loving toward her. We all want love and acceptance, especially when we are acting our worst. We know we're being bad, and we want to be loved anyway. I believe teens want this more than anything.

Grace and love trump punishment and pain. Parents do not need to move away from appropriate consequences or to lower their standards and accept bad behavior and broken rules. But they do need to love and accept their child right where he is, especially when he's at his worst.

Grace does not move away from accountability, but it always moves to embrace the offender.

LEARNING TO FORGIVE WHEN IT'S HARD

The example set by parents in the area of forgiveness is crucial to a child's development and is usually a character trait that is more caught than taught. If a parent holds a grudge when a child makes a mistake—big or small—the child learns that he is only worth loving when he does every-thing right. Ouch!

It's hard to forgive those who hurt you—even your kids—but forgiveness is vital for a family to stand strong against every storm. Forgiveness gives up hope that the past will ever change, but it keeps the faith that the future will be better and better. A parent's example and display of forgiveness will be a beacon of truth to his or her children.

When your heart has been broken, your values trashed, and your au-thority mocked, it is a tall order not to take it personally. Parents with ado-lescents who challenge them must constantly pray for their kids during the storm. I would suggest a daily "heart check" to pull out any roots of resent-ment and bitterness and remember to forgive.

Forgiveness in the world of teens is something that is given. True for-giveness can't be forced, taken, manufactured, or coerced. It comes from the heart but does not come naturally. The ability for teens to acknowledge that they have hurt someone comes with age, wisdom, and the viewing of a good example. As a parent, your focus must be on giving forgiveness to those you have hurt. Change the expectation that your child will look at you and say, "Will you forgive me for what I've done?" because you're not going to hear that often.

FORGETTING IS ESSENTIAL

To allow the pain of your child's struggle to interfere with your relationship only muddies the water. Expectations have to change or you will go crazy in the process, and you will ruin the relationship that you have greatly invested in.

It is essential that once forgiveness is given, the past must be forgotten. The past has an amazing way of clouding the future. So I don't ever bring it up. Sure, if there has been a pattern of behavior that is inappropriate, there needs to be a discussion about that habitual behavior. But it never does a parent good to bring up past events, decisions, and mistakes. Reminders of past mistakes only squelch the desire to make decisions and eliminate the possibility of change.

There are two comments that can shut down a child and move him to believing that if he can never change what he's done in the past, then there's no hope for relationship in the future. Those statements are used when you begin a sentence: "You always . . ." or "You never . . . ."

And here's the killer. Whenever you tell your child, "You'll never change," it kills hope that anything will ever be different.

DOING WHAT IS RIGHT WHEN YOUR CHILD IS DOING NOTHING BUT WRONG

Mom and Dad, nothing goes unnoticed. The times your child hurts you in the course of applying the truth learned from you in this crazy, mixed-up world does not get lost in the chaos. God knows when your child has hurt you. He understands disappointment, so find your strength in Him, not your kids. And dedicate yourself to forgiving the hurt your children cause in your life so that your relationship with them can flourish.

FOCUS EXERCISES

▌ KEY CONCEPTS

1. If one walks away from conflict feeling a sense of *winning*, then I'm sure that the other walks away *hurt*.

2. Learning to *love* when you've been *offended* is paramount in the relationships within a family.

3. It's called *grace* when you move toward an offender when that person has violated your *values*, *principles*, and *standards*.

4. Avoid issues *now*, and they will come *later* when they are much *bigger*, when consequences are usually *much greater*.

5. I know that if I *quit* and *give up*, the relationship *stops*, and the *hope* for anything in the future becomes *dim*.

6. *Grace* and *love* trump *punishment* and *pain*.

7. If you retract your *relationship* when your child messes up, you *invalidate* all you've been building, and all your good *intentions* of loving your child through the adolescent years will go *down the drain*.

8. *Forgiveness* in the world of teens is something that is *given*. True forgiveness can't be *forced, taken, manufactured, or coerced*. It comes from the *heart* but does not come *naturally*.

9. Whenever you tell your child, *"You'll never change,"* it kills *hope* that anything will ever be *different*.

QUESTIONS FOR DISCUSSION

1. Can you remember the last time your child hurt you through actions or comments that violated your values, principles, morals, or desires for your child? Why was it so hard to forgive when he or she did this to you?

2. If giving grace, moving toward your child when you have been violated, is so hard, did you really think it would feel good to do so?

3. What would it mean to you to have someone who has offended you, regardless of the amount of time that has passed, come up to you to apologize and ask for your forgiveness?

4. Is there someone in your life you have not forgiven? Do you avoid this person at all costs?

5. Is there someone in your life you have offended and have wronged? Do you avoid that person because you don't know how to ask for their forgiveness?

6. Do you think it is as hard on your child to know that you remember everything about the past as it is to have someone in your life who has taken into account all the wrongdoing that you have done?

7. Why do you think that it's so hard to ask for forgiveness (for what you have done) and to give forgiveness (for what others have done to you)?

8. If your children knew that you would still love them no matter what they've done, are doing, or will do to you, do you think this would strengthen your relationship or cause you to feel like a doormat?

■ ACTION POINT FOR THE WEEK

Chances are, there are people in your life who have done you wrong. Whether the mention of that person in third grade still causes you to feel a sting, or the person who divorced you soon after your college years still makes you feel an overwhelming sense of rejection and hurt, your movement toward that person when he or she doesn't really deserve it is an act of grace. And no matter how tough it is to make contact, be in this person's presence, or engage with him or her, it's important that you release the person from how he or she has hurt you.

You don't always have to use the words "I want you to know that I forgive you." Sometimes that can cause a war, a "who did what to whom" conversation that ignites a fire and might just burn more bridges. Sometimes, just a call, a conversation, a card in the mail, or a note that you were thinking of the person and just wanted to see how he or she was doing conveys a message of forgiveness in your willingness to be the first to make contact.

Now, do this—share two things with your kids around the dinner table or while you're riding in the car. One would be when you did something wrong to someone and asked forgiveness for your wrongdoing. The second would be sharing where someone did something to you and you gave forgiveness. Make sure you talk about where the relationships are today. The Christian life is more caught than taught, and never will there be a better lesson taught than when your kids see that you are capable of making mistakes, and also adept at forgiving others. This is how kids learn about forgiveness.

Session
9

TAKE A REGULAR BREAK

It's hard for any of us to walk into a setting where we know we're going to be criticized, isn't it? It's equally hard hearing that we should have done better or that we haven't performed up to our capabilities. And it's miserable to hear how we've disappointed those we love. Isn't that exactly what some tweens and teens experience *every day*—in school, in their social settings, and maybe even at home?

We all know, and may have experienced, the reality that constant criticism crushes excitement and enthusiasm and eventually ruins any type of commitment between relationships. So in time, you and I, as adults, can control our lives, go to the places that make us come alive, and stay away from those places that wear us out. If only kids could do the same. If attendance at school is critical and a retreat isn't possible, or peer relationships become unfavorable, most kids can't "opt out" for a better environment. They're stuck with what and where they are. When kids are in this position, it's hardly a good idea to make sure that home becomes that controlling, critical, and correcting environment.

Whether intended or unintentional, real or perceived, presented perfectly or mightily botched, criticism and correction charge a high price if their timing is the smallest feather that tips the scale, becomes too much of a good thing, and moves a child to become overwhelmed or feel a bit of overload.

In many cases, kids who feel besieged by the constant pressure of performance, fueling their anger and exacerbating their anxiety, begin to feel futile in their attempts to manage their intensified pressure. At those times kids withdraw and change their motto from "Be the best you can be" to "I can't do anything right."

I encourage parents to step into their adolescents' shoes and think about how hard it is to come home every day from doing their best not to get sucked into the cultural whirlpool, only to hear once again from their parents how they're not doing enough or not doing it right.

Have you ever wondered why kids can't wait to go hang out with friends, or become engrossed with a boyfriend or girlfriend, or hang out with the bad kids you don't want them hanging with? It's more than just socialization. I believe they're looking for *rest*. Have you ever scratched your head in curiosity wondering why many teens are consumed with media and video games or love to watch movies, read books, and get lost in fantasy? I think they're looking for a *getaway*. Have you been puzzled by the number of kids who smoke pot, get drunk on the weekends, don't have any motivation, or don't care about much? Sadly, many are looking for an *escape* from the pressures they experience in a culture that is counter to how they have been raised. While I don't agree with their behavior, I've come to understand it.

So, let's make our homes places of rest and eliminate the need for our kids to have to search beyond our homes to find what they so desperately need.

Most kids I know are looking for a place to have fun, to have a little excitement, and to have rest. My hope is that your home can become a place that provides an atmosphere of relationship that allows for fun, engages in something that is exciting, and provides a place of rest for your kids, a retreat from the pressures of their lives.

> Kids are going to find rest somewhere. I hope they find it in your home.

In a child's eyes upon entering the teen years, home can be viewed as a battlefield and a place where "rest" never happens. Teens come home from school, where they have worked hard to maintain the standard, uphold the principles, and stand for what is right against a tsunami of influence that is pushing against them telling them to be this, accept this lifestyle, try this stuff, look different, listen to this, say that, believe it all, don't listen to your parents . . . whew! Upon getting home they are pushed to clean their rooms, do their chores, feed the dog, study for an hour, get ready for piano, go to gymnastics, go to church, blah, blah, blah, blah. They are worn out! They need a break. They need rest. And if parents don't give it to them, teenagers will find ways to relieve the pressure that the world's influence is putting on them. Our homes should be places of rest.

Make your home a fun place.

MAKING YOUR HOME A PLACE OF REST

Parents must be intentional about creating a place of rest. This doesn't mean that you relax the boundaries and forget the rules that have been established in your home. You can allow some downtime within those boundaries by relaxing some expectations of cleanliness, tidiness, doing chores, sitting around, and watching sports or movies. I know many parents who were more concerned about high academic marks or the cleanliness of their child's room than the heart of their estranged high school graduate. These parents would now give anything to be able to do it all over again and lower the bar just a bit for the sake of relationship.

Why don't you commit to just correcting your kids on Monday, Wednesday, and Friday (don't tell them), not with the intent of letting them "get away with murder" but with the intent of helping home become a place of rest. This means that you just let the other days slip. Chances are, if your child "messes up" on Tuesday, he'll also mess up on Wednesday, one of your days of correction. Adapt a mind-set as a parent that you aren't going to comment on grades, correct bad habits, or criticize their remarks or comments. This doesn't mean that these "off" days become party days for your kids. But it does mean that you ignore the offense; you postpone the engagement until a later time. Quite honestly, I've found that this also allows you to reflect on the real problems, and after twenty-four hours you might just see that the concern you had for your child isn't that concerning the next day. This will force you to choose only the important things to correct and keep you from being a nag, or one who is always picking at his or her inconsistencies and inconsideration.

Kids need a connection.

Moms, if you always have a comment or a question ready to jump off your tongue at any moment, learn to speak half as much as you listen. Dads, spend time fixing the "rest problem" in your home and quit fixing everything else outside your home. If you're a grandparent, cut in half the number of comments you make about how everyone should know your better way to accomplish something. Everyone, be content with your investment in the lives of those around you and learn to "rest" in those relationships. Quit trying to always make everything "better"; this mind-set drives kids nuts.

MAKING YOUR HOME A PLACE WHERE YOUR KIDS FEEL CONNECTED

As time gets tight at home with everyone busier and life increasingly ticking at a faster pace with more activities, more commitments, and fuller schedules, the amount of time dedicated to correcting problems tends to remain the same. What gets squeezed out is the relational time. The verbal correcting of misdoings, shortcomings, and inappropriate behavior becomes priority to such a level that so much time and effort is spent correcting that there's very little time for connecting.

Kids are looking for connections. And what better connections to make than those with your own kids? Here's another idea: have a weekly joke night at your home. Tell everyone that they must come to the table and bring a clean joke they found on the Internet. The purpose is to make others laugh. A family that laughs together . . . has a good time. And don't always make something spiritual out of it. Relax, have a good time, and make sure your kids go to bed at night saying, "I had a good time with my parents tonight."

———— FOCUS EXERCISES ————

KEY CONCEPTS

1. It's hard being *criticized*, hearing that we should have done better, and being *reminded* that we haven't performed up to our *capabilities*.

2. *Constant criticism crushes* excitement and enthusiasm, and eventually ruins any type of commitment in relationships.

3. Too much of a good thing moves a child to become *overwhelmed* or feel a bit of *overload*.

4. Change their motto from "Be the best you can be" to "I can't do anything right."

5. Teens are *worn out*! They need a *break*. They need *rest*. And if they don't get it at home, kids will find it *elsewhere*.

6. With *fuller* schedules, the amount of time dedicated to correcting problems tends to remain the same. What gets squeezed out is the *relational time*.

7. Relax, have a good time, and make sure your kids go to bed at night saying, *"I had a good time with my parents tonight."*

▍ QUESTIONS FOR DISCUSSION

1. Do you have a day at your home when everyone can rest, recover, and be refreshed?

2. Do you allow your kids to sleep in and catch up on their rest on weekends and holidays?

3. Do you allow your kids the opportunity to do nothing at times?

4. When is the last time your family had a relaxing night at home?

5. What is it about you that brings relaxation to the family, and what would your kids say you do that causes tension and strain within the home?

6. Have you determined you can never rest and always have to be on the move, fixing something, rather than sitting down and just enjoying the opportunity to do nothing? Why?

7. Would your kids say that you are uptight or relaxed?

8. What do they feel when they are around you?

9. If you have a hard time sitting down and relaxing, how will your kids ever discover how to do the same?

10. If you could change one thing about how you engage with your kids, what would it be?

11. How would you like your relationship with your tweens and teens to look different from how it does now?

■ ACTION POINT FOR THE WEEK

Relax this week. Pull back on the push for academics. Lighten up the correction for a few days. And if something goes wrong, don't confront. Just let it slide for a week. And then see if the relationship with your child gets better. Chances are, it will. Then the challenge is to introduce new ways of correcting, confronting, and giving consequences.

Creating a place where your child can find rest is far more important than the difference between a "C" and an "A" on a report card, participation in a particular sport, or having to fulfill a particular requirement by parents. I'm not saying that good grades, sports, and parental requirements aren't important; it's just that there may be some other items that are *more* important.

——— CONCLUSION ———

FAMILY — THE PERMANENT HARBOR IN A CONSTANT STORM

Parenting is a lot like putting together a puzzle. Most parents spend the first twelve years of a child's life assembling the edge pieces in order to build the boundaries, and then they start filling in the picture with what is familiar. They spend the next six to ten years tackling the unknown colors and pieces, trying to figure out where they go and how they all fit. The challenge is usually the latter, not the former.

But there's another essential part of the parenting puzzle. If you don't understand this, you might have the tendency to delay the finishing of your puzzle to a later time. This part has to do with the colors.

Simply put, if it were not for the dark and jagged pieces that seemingly have no purpose, the puzzle would not become the masterpiece it was created to be. The dark pieces are just as much a part of the puzzle as the brightly colored and rounded pieces, as their complementary relationships with one another highlight and accent the bigger picture's beauty. It's the good and the bad melded together that brings about the goodness of relationships as God intended. This is the bigger picture view of parenting, and it's essential.

Because of the big-picture plan for your family, I encourage you to invest your time, effort, and resources into the relationships around you that count and not get bogged down in minor stuff that will eventually pass. Your kids are faced with things that you and I never thought would even exist. And they're exposed to things that most of us didn't get exposed to until much later in life. The confusion of media bombardment, gender issues, and living in a time of uncertainty all have a tendency to pull your kids away from you in their preteen and teenage years. They need you to help them get through their confusion and mature into healthy adults.

It sounds like it's going to be a hard trek, doesn't it? While I believe that if we're not involved in the life of our kids they'll surely have a tough time, I also believe that there's hope and opportunity to raise good kids who are responsible, mature, and motivated for the challenges of adulthood that lie ahead.

I truly believe that by utilizing the same styles and techniques that I use in my work with teens at our ranch, parents can offer their kids something they'll never get anywhere else—a relationship that provides a connection that is unlike any other.

If I could encapsulate everything we've done in this series in one paragraph, I would say this:

This world is tough on kids. Its confusing culture is reflected in the heightened strength and energy in a teen's questioning of traditional values and principles. Lack of respect, uncertainty, overexposure, and confusion about issues surrounding gender have only escalated the great disconnect in relationships among teens, ushering in a world of performance and appearance. So parents must shift their styles of parenting from ideologies of perfection, signs of judgment, and shows of authority to a relational style that walks alongside a child rather than dictates from above. That new style would involve, and not be limited to, putting the relationship first in the life of your children. They need you more than ever.

Your drama queen and tough guy are worth the investment of your life, even when you don't understand where a certain piece of the puzzle fits. I'm convinced of this: you are just as much a part of their puzzles as they are of yours. There are many puzzles on the table within your family, and their uniqueness is as exceptional and exclusive as a falling snowflake or your unique fingerprints.

May your family be blessed as you parent your children through their teenage years. I'm sure one day you'll laugh at the antics of your drama queen. And you'll marvel at your tough guy as he finishes his chapter of adolescence and moves into adulthood.

In the process, enjoy the puzzle!

APPENDIX A – CONVERSATION STARTERS

Here are some questions to start a conversation with your teenager. Remember, ask the question and don't give an answer unless he or she asks you. And don't share your opinion about kids' answers; their answers will give insight into their lives. Don't do anything to shut down their responses. These are great for around-the-table discussions, while you're riding in the car, or when you're traveling together.

- What's something about our family that sticks out the most in your mind?

- If you could change one thing about yourself, what would it be?

- If you could change one thing about our family, what would it be?

- If you could change one thing about me, what would it be?

- What causes the most fear in your life?

- What's the most fun thing you've ever done?

- Am I really as bad as you think I am?

- Do you think that we're the only people out of all the solar systems known to man?

- What is one thing that I could do for you to make your life better?

- If there were one person in the world that you wish would give you a call, who would it be and what do you think you'd talk about?

- We're all known for something. What would you like to be known for?

- Do you find yourself doing things that you don't want to do, and not doing the things you want to do?

- What would someone in your class who doesn't know you say about you after watching you?

- Who is the most talented musician you've ever heard? Do you think you'll be listening to him or her ten years from now?

- Do you think all people have the capability of being famous?

- Do you think that you'll be famous one day? If so, what for? If not, why not?

- Do you think dogs hear everything we say and hide their feelings well, or do they see us at our worst and just decide to love us anyway?

- When is a friend a real friend, and when is one not?

- How many times have you been hurt this past month? What was it that hurt the most?

- What one word would you use to describe our family?

- If you won the lotto jackpot, and had to spend it all, what would you spend it on?

- Out of all the teachers you've ever had, which one do you remember the most, and why?

- What talent would you like to have that you don't?

- How much money would you have to be given to shave your head?

- Do you think everyone on *American Idol* is really that good?

- Are you more likely to talk on your phone or send texts?

- What do you think it means to have a spirit of excellence in the way you work?

- What's the weirdest thing that you've ever seen on the Internet?

- What do you think the perfect woman would look like?

- What's the coolest looking mustache you've ever seen?

- If you could spend one week on vacation at a place of your choice and you could take one person with you, where would it be and who would you take?

- When was the last time you laughed out loud, and what made you laugh?

- If you could sit down and eat a meal with one person in the world, who would it be?

- Do you ever have a hard time taking what you know to be true into the world that you live in?

- Who's the weirdest person you know? Is there anything about this person that is just like you?

- What would be the first thing you'd do if the sun didn't come up tomorrow?

- What do you think is the biggest controversy happening in the world today?

- Do you think that you're too fat, too tall, too skinny, too short, or have the wrong color hair?

- Is there a disease you would never want to die from?

- If you were an animal, what kind of animal would you want to be? Why?

- Who's the greatest sports hero of all time?

- Do you think it's important to always have to share your opinion, and what do you think of people who do?

- What's the neatest website you've ever visited?

- Do you think the music you listen to influences you, or is it just an expression of what you feel?

- Which is better: having a great family or having a lot of money?

- Who's your closest friend, and what one wish would you wish for that friend?

- Why do you think that just about all men on television sitcoms are portrayed as buffoons?

- Do you think that you would talk more if you texted less?

- Do you think that social media sites are true to life, or are they a little fake? What one word would you use to describe people who are always on these sites?

- What would make school mean more to you?

- If a tornado was coming toward your home and you had time to grab only one thing before you protected yourself in a cellar, what would you take?

- What's your favorite movie of all time? What's so special about it?

- Would you rather be rich and have as much money as you'll ever need, or have everyone think you're the kindest and most helpful person they've ever met?

- What is the favorite meal of the person sitting next to you?

- Would you rather travel cross-country in a covered wagon or fly around the universe in a space shuttle?

- Do you have a special talent that others don't know about?

- Who is your best friend and why?

- What's the funniest joke you've ever heard? Will you tell it?

- What is the worst food you've ever eaten at school?

- Do you think there are people in the world that have never made a mistake?

- Would you ever jump out of an airplane with a parachute or hop off a bridge on a bungee rope?

- Do you remember where you were when you heard of the greatest tragedy? What was the tragedy, and what were you doing when you heard the news?

- What do you miss the most about [insert name of someone he or she knows who has died]?

- How is this year in school different from your last year in school?

- What actor or actress would you want to be like?

- What do you think is the greatest thing that's ever been done? What is the greatest thing that you've ever done?

- Which are better: tattoos or piercings?

- What's a lesson about life that you've learned this week?

- If you could have plastic surgery on one part of your body, what would it be and why?

- If you could see someone in concert and sit on the first row, who would it be?

- When you hear someone talk about a "real man," who comes to your mind?

APPENDIX B – HOW TO DISCUSS CONFLICT

The goal of investing one week's time into a one-on-one weekly meeting with your child is to create a place, time, and opportunity for you and your child to discuss any conflict, potential or current. These are some discussion starters:

- Sweetheart, your mom and I don't think it's time for you to get a cell phone just yet. I know others in your class have them. You're thirteen, and we've always said that you can have one when you're fifteen. I'm willing to back that up to fourteen. Is that a good compromise for you?

- Your dad and I think that it's best that you not spend the night at your friend's house yet. He's more than welcome to come here for the night, but we're not comfortable with you there until we meet his parents. Do you think they would call us or we could drop by to meet them sometime?

- I see some things that concern me about your use of the Internet. I looked at the Internet history and saw that you've been spending some time on some porn sites that aren't appropriate. Let's figure out what to do to make sure this doesn't become a problem.

- I think you and I disagree on something that's important to talk about. It's about the amount of time you spend playing video games. It seems like that's all you want to do, and you seem to be spending more time playing than we agreed to. Let's talk about what solutions we can find to this problem. Do you think it's a problem?

- I'm struggling with the way you treat your mom. For the most part, it seems like you're mad at her all the time and treat her with a great deal of disrespect. Let's talk about what Mom's doing wrong in her approach to you, and then let's talk about what you're doing wrong in your approach to her. I love your mom, and I know you do too. Do you think we can come to some agreement on how we're going to live respectfully together in our home?

- I'm not sure about this one friend of yours. It seems as though every time you're with her, you get in trouble at school, or when you two get together, you start to be negative. Now, I don't want to pick your friends for you, but I also don't want you to get in trouble at school or become negative. We want to get to know her better. Could she come over for dinner and let us get to know her?

- I've spent some time thinking about what we talked about last week. Considering what you said, what your mom has told me, and the conclusion I've come to, we're not going to let you go on the spring break trip you asked us about. Unless you can convince me otherwise this morning, I'm going to have to stick with my decision. So give it your best shot, and let's see if you can get me to change my mind.

- Is there anything that's happening now that you think might be a conflict between us in the future? Your mom heard some things, and I checked them out with some other parents, and they've all said the same thing. Anything you think we need to talk about this morning?

- I know that we've set the rules at home and you're having a tough time with a couple of them. Let's talk about those. But first, do you understand the reason we've set up these rules for our home? Then, is there a reason that you're having a tough time following them?

- Hey, you're almost eighteen. How can I help you make this next transition in life without wrecking the way we operate in our home?

- I want to be the kind of father (or mother) you want me to be. I'm not sure that I understand what that looks like, and I'm not sure how to get there, but I would love to discuss this and not be afraid to make changes. Are you game to talk about this?

- Look, I know you want to finish the eighth grade and move on to high school. I also know that the way you're headed, that just isn't going to happen. Let's talk about what I can do to help you accomplish what you want. Can we do that?

- You've been playing soccer for the last five years, and it sure seems that you've loved it. Help me understand why you want to give it up now, after you've committed to play this next year.

- I know that your sister (brother) can drive you nuts. I had a brother (sister) like that when I was growing up. And just as my brother has turned out to be a pretty good guy, I'm sure your sister will also. I just want to make sure that you don't kill each other before you have the chance to turn out to be pretty good, as well. What can I do to ensure that the fighting stops so that there can be some harmony in our home?

- You know that I can't stand your music. You also know that I'm not going to play music police—that's not one of the things I signed up for when becoming a parent. So, I'm giving you this portable music player with ear buds so you can keep your music to yourself in hopes that my migraines will stop. Can you help me not die prematurely by not blaring your music through the house?

- You know your mother and I don't get along well. And she dislikes me more since I got remarried. But she is your mother, and I'm asking you to not take out your anger towards me on her. She's trying the best she can. Can you help her in her house, and can you promise to discuss with me any anger that you have for me?

- I blew it and made a huge mistake. I want to say I'm sorry for what I've done, and I want to ask you to forgive me. Is there anything I can do to make our relationship right? I want to have a good relationship; I'm tired of not getting along.

ABOUT THE AUTHOR

Mark Gregston is the founder and executive director of Heartlight, a residential counseling center for teens located in Longview, Texas, where he lives with sixty high school kids from around the country. He is also the host of *Parenting Today's Teens*, a daily and weekend radio program heard on over fourteen hundred radio outlets, helping parents across North America navigate through the turbulent waters of their child's adolescence. He is a popular speaker and author, combining humor and stories with insights and wisdom gained from his thirty-eight years of working with teens and parents, and spends almost every weekend of the year leading a parenting seminar in various cities.

Mark has been married for thirty-eight years to his high school sweetheart, Jan, who has tolerated his crazy schedule of working with kids. They have two kids, three grandkids, one dog, one cat, four llamas, and way too many horses.

Heartlight Ministries is a Christian residential counseling and schooling opportunity dedicated to helping teens and their families work through difficult situations.

Heartlight strives to provide the very best care to families caught in crisis situations that require an adolescent's removal from the home. Our co-ed, year-round program accommodates 60 residents.

We are committed to the belief that an atmosphere of relationships creates an arena for change.

HeartlightMinistries
ESTABLISHED 1988

903.668.2173   866.700.FAMILY   WWW.HEARTLIGHTMINISTRIES.ORG